Contents

chapter four

Hansel and Gretel

photocopiable activities

chapter five

The Emperor's New Clothes

Anyone who has worked with young children will notice how much time they spend just standing and staring. They are not being rude, they are simply watching. This is how they learn – copying others enables them to work out their own methods and ideas, making their own discoveries and building their self-confidence and self-image. To promote this type of learning we need to give them a rich variety of things to do and make that will stimulate their curiosity, develop their language and numeracy, increase their physical abilities and foster social skills. This book of traditional story activities provides children with these opportunities.

Getting ready for school

The activities support the *Desirable Outcomes for Children's Learning* identified by the School Curriculum and Assessment Authority. Although the National Curriculum is not mandatory for pre-school and Reception class children, this book will prepare them for the time when Level I needs to be implemented. The activity pages in each chapter focus on a subject area of the National Curriculum/Scottish Guidelines 5–14: two for English, two for mathematics and one each for science, design and technology, history, geography, art, music, PE and RE. Each chapter also contains display ideas and a cookery activity.

Traditional stories

The activities are presented in five chapters based on the following stories: The Enormous Turnip, The Gingerbread Man, Rapunzel, Hansel and Gretel and The Emperor's New Clothes. These stories may be new to some children, but not for long, because they will be requested over and over again. Traditional stories have stood the test of time and have been handed down from generation to generation. They are our heritage and we owe it to our children to pass them on.

Many of the stories are frightening and cruel and illustrate undesirable traits of human behaviour. Some adults may think that they should not be told to young children, but Freud maintained that such stories are very important for the psyche of our children. The psychologist Bruno Bettelheim explained why this is so. He said that children often have deep fears and anxieties that they cannot explain. When they recognise these feelings in stories, they can project them on to the evil characters. This helps them to cope with their anxieties and come to terms with them. Children can be reassured, however, that for every 'baddy' there is a 'goody' who is more powerful! And even when things don't turn out too well we can always hope. Hope is part of the magic and excitement of life.

Using this book

The introductory page of each chapter gives a condensed version of the story. Try to tell it rather than read it. You don't have to be word perfect – if you alter or forget anything, you can rest assured that there will be plenty of little people to correct you!

For each activity there is a list of what is needed. Preparation is kept to a minimum and can often be done by the older children in the group. There are clear instructions on what to do, and illustrations and diagrams for clarification. The discussion section helps the children to connect the activities to the main story. This section also includes appropriate points of general knowledge. Suggestions are made on how activities may be adapted for younger children or extended for older ones. Finally, the follow up activities on each page are cross-curricular.

Each chapter provides two photocopiable pages at the end of the book which include sequencing and matching tasks and board games. They relate to the traditional stories and are used either in the main or follow-up activity.

The two display activities towards the end of each chapter often use the work that the children have produced on the previous activities pages. It is intended that these displays should be interactive and used for further learning.

Although it is not necessary to work through the stories or the activities within the chapters in a specific order, it will be less confusing for the children to complete one story chapter before starting another.

Group sizes have been stated but these are only recommendations since the practitioner will know what is appropriate for his or her own group. It will often be more practical to tell the whole group what you are going to be doing and why, and then to let an adult helper take a small group to complete the task. Whichever way is chosen, hopefully this book will introduce children to the joy of traditional stories and provide them with stimulating sources of activity.

Cookery

Each chapter contains a cookery activity related to the 'theme' which allows the children to prepare food that they can eat.

Establish a regular hygiene routine before any cookery activity, making sure all children wear a protective apron and wash their hands thoroughly. Be sensitive to individual children's cultural or religious customs, and practices such as vegetarianism which will limit the consumption of some foods. Ensure that you and the other staff are aware of any food allergies, intolerances or special dietary requirements. Finally, make sure the children help you to clear everything away.

Links with home

The School Curriculum and Assessment Authority stresses the role of 'Parents as partners' in the education of their children. This is especially important when children are first separated from their parents for a short time. This book provides an excellent opportunity to involve parents because many of them will already be familiar with the stories. It may be a good idea to make an enlarged copy of the current story you are focusing on and to pin it up where parents can read it. This will help them to predict the kind of questions their children may ask and also to smooth out any anxieties which the stories may promote, especially the stories which include wicked characters. If the parents are willing to give you feedback, this will enable you to assess how much the children are understanding and enjoying their tasks. In this way there can be a two-way dialogue of the capabilities and progress of the children.

chapter one
▶ introduction ◀

The Enormous Turnip

A turnip is only a common-place vegetable so we can imagine the surprise of the little old man and the little old woman when it grew to a spectacular size. This story emphasises the problems of just such an unusual event and shows a way of solving it through determination and co-operation.

Once upon a time there was a little old man and a little old woman who wanted to grow vegetables. They dug some compost into the soil and sowed some turnip seeds. In no time at all there were little green shoots pushing up through the soil in neat tidy rows. The old man and woman were terribly excited.

Now just like children grow differently, so do turnips. One grew twice as big as the others, then four times as big and then eight times as big. It just grew and grew until it was enormous. 'Time to pull it up!' said the little old man, and he took hold of the leaves and gave them a tug. Nothing happened, so he beckoned to his wife for help. The little old woman pulled the little old man and the little old man pulled the turnip but it wouldn't budge.

The little old woman called to a boy cycling past, 'Can you lend a hand?' So the boy pulled the little old woman, the little old woman pulled the little old man and the little old man pulled the turnip. It wouldn't budge.

The boy shouted to a girl walking her dog, 'Come and help us!' The girl pulled the boy, the boy pulled the little old woman, the little old woman pulled the little old man and the little old man pulled the turnip. It just wouldn't budge.

'I'll get the dog,' said the girl. The dog pulled the girl, the girl pulled the boy, the boy pulled the little old woman, the little old woman pulled the little old man and the little old man pulled the turnip. It still wouldn't budge.

The dog spied a cat and barked for it to come and help. The cat pulled the dog, the dog pulled the girl, the girl pulled the boy, the boy pulled the little old woman, the little old woman pulled the little old man and the little old man pulled the turnip. Nothing would make it budge.

The cat spotted a mouse and mewed for its help. The mouse pulled the cat, the cat pulled the dog, the dog pulled the girl, the girl pulled the boy, the boy pulled the little old woman, the little old woman pulled the little old man and the little old man pulled the turnip. That did it – the soil cracked open, the turnip budged and down everyone fell.

Later they all shared some turnip stew. It was delicious!

Starting with story
Traditional story activities

Who's pulling?

Objective
English – to develop descriptive skills and to increase vocabulary.

Group size
Whole group.

What you need
A teddy bear, a construction brick, a chair, a pencil.

What to do
Hold up the teddy and ask the children to describe it. (Brown, soft, furry, beady-eyed, a toy.) Do the same with the brick, the chair and the pencil. Remind the children of the story of 'The Enormous Turnip' and see if they can guess from the following descriptive riddles who is doing the pulling.

I have four legs, a coat of fur, long sharp claws and I love to purr. (Cat.)

I wag my tail and sometimes bark. I always guard your house when dark. (Dog.)

I'm beady-eyed, long-tailed and small – I wouldn't hurt you, 'No, not at all!' (Mouse.)

It's round and white and can be eaten. It's full of goodness, can't be beaten. (Turnip.)

My hair is grey, my voice is deep, I often snore when I'm asleep. (Old man or woman!)

I'm not a diamond or a pearl – to guess me right I rhyme with curl. (Girl.)

Discussion
When you describe something you talk about its size, shape, colour, hardness or softness, its use, its age and other things. Why don't we say everything about people when we describe them? Explain that it can be rude to describe someone as very fat or very ugly and we should always try to find something kind to say about people. How do blind people manage to describe things when they can't see? (By touch.)

For younger children
Allow the children to feel the different objects to help them describe them.

For older children
Let them help you to make up riddles about the boy and any other creatures who might have helped pull up the turnip (donkey, sheep, hedgehog, worm).

Follow-up activities
▲ Put some small items into a 'feely' bag. Ask the children to describe what they can feel, like a blind person would.
▲ Play a game of 'I spy' using the initial sound of the article as a clue.
▲ Describe an object and count how many different things you can say about it.

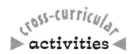

'T' for turnip

Objective
English – to recognise initial sounds and to draw a vegetable alphabet.

Group size
Whole group.

What you need
An assortment of as many vegetables as you can manage including a turnip, a book on growing vegetables which has pictures, such as *The New Vegetable and Herb Expert* by DG Hessayon (Expert Books), a large sheet of card, a black marker pen.

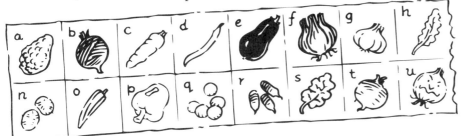

Preparation
Divide the card up into 26 squares. Mark the top left-hand corner of each square with a letter of the alphabet written in alphabetical order. Pin this alphabet card up so that the children can see as you draw on it.

What to do
Hold up the turnip and ask the children what it is and what sound it begins with. Draw a picture of the turnip shape in the appropriate square on the alphabet card. Repeat this with all the vegetables you have collected. Ask the children to suggest vegetables which can be drawn in the unfilled squares. A list might include avocado, beetroot, carrot, dwarf bean, eggplant (aubergine), fennel, garlic, horseradish, Indian corn (sweet corn), Jerusalem artichoke, kidney bean, lettuce, mint, new potatoes, okra, pepper, radish, spinach, turnip, vegetable marrow, winter cabbage, yam (sweet potato), zucchini (courgette). Make up funny pictures and names for the awkward letters such as Quite big peas, Ugly onions, Xmas sprouts.

Discussion
Some vegetables grow under the ground and are called root vegetables. Can the children give you the names of some other root vegetables? Which vegetables grow as climbing plants? (Peas, beans, marrows, cucumbers.) Some vegetables can only grow in very hot countries. Avocados need tropical conditions.

For younger children
Let them colour the outline drawings on photocopiable page 87 using the appropriate colours.

For older children
Each time you introduce a new vegetable sound ask a child to come and point to the correct letter square on the card.

Follow-up activities
▲ Give each child a copy of photocopiable page 87 to write in the initial letter of the vegetables.
▲ Ask the children to give an example of a red, a green, a yellow, a white and a brown vegetable.
▲ Talk about which vegetables can be eaten raw and which need cooking.
▲ Make a group survey of favourite vegetables to eat.

Which order?

Objective
Mathematics – to sequence pictures and to introduce ordinal numbers.

Group size
Six children.

What you need
Seven copies of photocopiable page 88, felt-tipped pens or crayons, paper-clips.

Preparation
Cut up six of the sheets into their separate pictures and arrange each set in random order before securing with a paper-clip.

What to do
Hold up a copy of photocopiable page 88 and discuss each picture with the children. Count with them how many characters each picture has. Refer to each picture as the first, second, third and so on.

Give each child a set of pictures. Ask them to find the first picture from the story and place it in front of them to the top left, then to put the second picture to the right of the first one, and the third picture next to the second, gradually arranging all eight pictures in sequence.

Discussion
What is the first thing the children do each morning when they get up? There will be lots of different answers and some will obviously not be the first thing! Make use of this by emphasising that maybe it is the second or third thing that they do. What is the first thing they do when they arrive at your group? What is the last thing they do before they go to bed at night?

For younger children
Provide them with an uncut copy of photocopiable page 88 and let them place a counter on each new character.

For older children
Ask them to write the terms 1st, 2nd, 3rd, 4th, 5th, 6th, 7th and 8th on the appropriate pictures.

Follow-up activities
▲ Number some paper floor mats 1st, 2nd, 3rd, 4th, 5th. Ask individual children to step on the 1st mat or the 5th mat, and so on.
▲ Ask the children to sit on a row of chairs. Point out the first chair and ask them to say which seat they are sitting on (the third or fourth and so on).
▲ Make some ribbon rosettes – 1st, 2nd, 3rd – similar to those awarded at horse or flower shows. Award them to the smartest teddies or dolls!

▲ 10
Starting with story
Traditional story activities

Bigger and bigger

Objective
Mathematics – to appreciate that size alters with growth.

Group size
Six children.

What you need
A fresh turnip or a picture of one from a vegetable gardening book, sheets of A4 paper, a pencil and green crayon for each child.

What to do
Remind the children of the part of the story where 'One grew twice as big as the others, then four times as big and then eight times as big'. Give them each a piece of paper to fold in half and press the crease. Fold it in half again and repeat this procedure twice more (makes 16 small feint squares). On the top fold of paper ask the children to draw a turnip and give it green leaves, then open up one fold of paper and draw another turnip which is twice as big as the first. When the next fold has been opened the children will be able to draw a turnip which is four times as big as the first. Opening the next fold will mean that the turnip can be drawn eight times as big. Finally, when the paper is fully unfolded they can draw an enormous turnip (see diagram). The children can now see the progressive growth of their turnip.

Discussion
When things grow they get bigger. Do the children realise that they are growing and getting bigger all the time? Can they compare their size to younger brothers or sisters? How can they tell that they are growing all the time? (Hair and nails need cutting frequently.) What things do they need to help them to grow? (Food, water, care.) Turnips get their food from the soil and their water from the rain.

For younger children
Fold their paper first for them and then let them re-fold it by following the creases.

For older children
Show them how to number the turnips in size order. Write number one on the smallest.

Follow-up activities
▲ Repeat the folding activity, this time drawing a carrot.
▲ Cut an apple into half and then one of the halves into quarters. Arrange all the pieces in size order.
▲ Ask the children to line up with the smallest child first and the tallest last.
▲ Arrange some home-grown tomatoes in size order and compare them to a packet of tomatoes bought from a supermarket – can these be put in size order?

Off the top

Objective
Science – to find out what plants need to grow, and to grow a turnip top.

Group size
Six children.

What you need
Seven raw turnips (with a lot of top and root left on if possible), seven saucers, a sharp knife and cutting board, at least one magnifying glass, a jug of water, seven labelling cards and pencils.

What to do
Give each child a turnip to examine with the magnifying glass then ask them to cut a 2cm slice off the top (closely supervised) and put this top, flat side down, into a saucer. Then they can pour a little water into the saucer and write their name and the date on a label to put next to the saucer. Cut the seventh turnip top and leave it in a saucer without water. Label it and put all the saucers in a warm, light place making sure that the water is kept topped up. After four or five days, if the children look through the magnifying glass they will see that leaves have started to sprout from all the turnip tops except the one without water.

Discussion
What did the children notice on their whole turnip? The turnip itself is a root – what other root vegetables can be eaten? (Beetroot, parsnip, carrot, swede.) What happened to the turnip top that was left without any water? Plants must have water, food and light to grow. The turnip uses its own main root as food. Usually root vegetables grow underground but they still need sunlight to grow their green leaves. Although a potato grows underground it is not a root but is a fat stem.

For younger children
Cut the turnip slice off for them. Instead of writing a name label let them do a little drawing which they can recognise as their own.

For older children
Write a daily account of what is happening to their turnip top. When it grows leaves they can record the leaf height.

Follow-up activities
▲ Grow tops cut from other root vegetables. Compare their rate of growth.
▲ Cover one of the growing turnip tops with newspaper. Does it still grow? What colour are its leaves?

Pull and push

Objective
Design and Technology – to design and make a pull and push turnip toy.

Group size
Six children.

What you need
A piece of thick black paper (14cm x 22cm) and a piece of thick white paper (20cm x 12cm) for each child, a craft knife, scissors, stapler, pencils and green crayons, a real turnip with leaves if possible.

Preparation
Cut the black and white paper into the sizes given above.

What to do
Show the children the turnip and explain that they are going to make a turnip toy that can be pulled out of the 'soil'. Ask them to draw a turnip on the white paper – with very big leaves that are wider than the turnip root. Let the children cut round the outline and colour the leaves and part of the turnip root green. Fold the black paper in half, and ask the children how much needs to be cut from along the fold to form a slot for the turnip. Cut it for them and ask them to place the turnip into the slot so that its leaves just peep out of the top of the 'soil'. Its root should poke out at the bottom (see diagram). Staple the two corners of the black paper and let the children play with

the turnip toy, pulling it out of the 'soil' and pushing it back again.

Discussion
What is the opposite of pulling? Do the children think that a turnip could be pushed back into the soil again? Once a ripe vegetable has been pulled up it is unlikely that it can continue growing even if it is dug back into the soil. Where do you see the words 'push' and 'pull' written? (Doors of shops.) What other opposite words do you know? (Up/down, in/out, front/back.)

For younger children
Give the children a pre-cut turnip to colour and show them how to place the turnip in the slot.

For older children
Write a little message on the turnip, which will be revealed when it is pulled out of the 'soil'.

Follow-up activities
▲ Make 'push' and 'pull' cards to stick on either side of a door.
▲ Play on a see-saw, saying 'up' and 'down' at the right time.
▲ Sort strands of knitting wool into opposites – long and short or thick and thin.

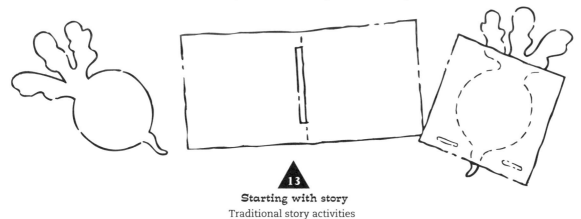

Stacks and stacks

Objective
History – to find out how harvesting methods have changed.

Group size
Six children.

What you need
A book on farming which has good pictures of harvesting machines, such as Dorling Kindersley's Eyewitness Guide *Farm* by Ned Halley, scissors, string, some hay or straw from a pet shop (sold in bags for rabbits) – if this is not available you could use Artstraws.

Preparation
Cut the string into 50cm lengths.

What to do
Ask the children to take a handful of the hay and fold it into a rectangular shape, perhaps rearranging some of the pieces to lie in the same direction. When their bundle is compact, they can wrap the string round it then tie it in a knot. With the scissors, show the children how to cut some hay off each end of the bundles so that it resembles a hay bale of approximately 5cm x 10cm. Make several mini-bales of hay. Look at and discuss pictures of modern farm machinery in a picture book.

Discussion
In the story the old man tried to pull the turnip up out of the soil by hand. Why wouldn't the turnip come up? (The roots had grown too deep.) What other way could he have got the turnip up? Would a spade have been strong enough? In the past, farmers had to do everything by hand – even the grass had to be cut by hand with a scythe. It was then left to dry before being bundled into bales of hay. What do farmers use nowadays to cut the grass in their fields? Tractor-drawn mowers and baling machines (as shown in the picture book) will cut, gather and bale the hay. Bales make hay easier to store or transport to market.

For younger children
Help younger children to secure their bundles with an elastic band.

For older children
Help them to build the bales into a haystack that will be stable. Compare it to building a wall with construction bricks.

Follow-up activities
▲ Smell the hay and say what it reminds you of. (Grass?)
▲ Play the game 'The farmer's in his den', found in *This Little Puffin...* compiled by Elizabeth Matterson (Puffin).
▲ Using the construction toys, invent and build a machine which could be used by a farmer.
▲ Sing the nursery rhyme 'Little Boy Blue'.

▲ 14
Starting with story
Traditional story activities

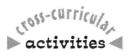
Worming along

Objective
Geography – to find out about earthworms and to make a wormery.

Group size
Small group.

What you need
A very large clear plastic jar or a small fish tank which will do for the wormery, carrier bags full of sand, of soil and of fallen leaves. A newspaper, a piece of thick dark cloth which will completely cover your wormery, a trowel and bucket, approximately a dozen worms.

Preparation
Collect worms from where they hide under stones and plant pots. Keep them in a small bucket of soil until you are ready.

What to do
Allow the children to examine and feel the worms, soil, sand and leaf matter. Layer the soil, newspaper (torn into small pieces), sand and leaves to come within 5cm of the top of the wormery. End with a layer of leaves and put the earthworms on top. Watch how they move and then cover the wormery with the thick dark cloth (earthworms do not like the light). Two days later remove the cloth and see what has happened inside. After a few days when you have finished your study, tip the contents of the wormery back into the garden. Ensure that the soil isn't too dry or too wet.

Discussion
Why did the turnip grow so large? (The earthworms made the soil suitable for vegetables to grow.) While worms burrow down into the soil looking for food they drag leaves with them, and make tunnels which let in air. This helps to keep the soil light and crumbly. How do earthworms move? (Their bodies are slippery and slimy and are made of lots of segments.) This means that they can pull themselves along in wriggles!

For younger children
In autumn young children will enjoy gathering fallen leaves for the wormery.

For older children
Take them into the garden and let them dig for worms.

Follow-up activities
▲ Examine the worms on a table through a magnifying glass. Try and count the segments!
▲ Study how worms move and let the children wriggle across the floor in the same way.
▲ Sing 'There's a worm at the bottom of my garden' in *This Little Puffin...* compiled by Elizabeth Matterson (Puffin).
▲ Use chalk to draw the different layers in the wormery. Drag a wetted finger up and down the layers to show the path of a worm.

A vegetable garden

Objective
Art – to make vegetable prints in the style of a vegetable garden.

Group size
Six children.

What you need
A selection of vegetables such as a turnip, parsnip, carrot, potato, cauliflower, cabbage, peppers, celery, mushrooms, sprouts, pea and bean pods, courgette, radish, sweetcorn. A large piece of painting paper for each child, a ruler, thick pencil, ready mixed different-coloured thick paints. Pieces of rubber or sponge (dampened) and empty food containers for print-pads (see preparation), layers of newspaper, a knife.

Preparation
Draw lines approximately 5cm apart on the painting paper, for vegetable rows. Fit the damp, foam rubber pieces into the containers to make print pads and pour a generous amount of paint onto each.

What to do
Let the children handle and smell the vegetables before cutting them into chunks suitable for printing (supervise the use of the knife). Rest the painting paper on a wad of newspaper, for a better print. Explain that the vegetables are to be printed in rows on the paper to look like a vegetable garden. Show them how to press a vegetable chunk onto the print pad and then print it on their paper several times carefully in a row. They can print another row with a different vegetable. Keep each vegetable piece to its own colour pad.

Discussion
Why do people who grow vegetables usually sow the seeds in rows? (A straight line of vegetable seedlings are easier to distinguish from weed seedlings.) What happens if vegetables are grown too closely together? They need plenty of room to grow big and healthy. How much room was left for the enormous turnip to grow?

For younger children
Allow them to print anywhere on the paper without confining them to the rows.

For older children
Let them choose how they would like to cut the vegetable pieces – lengthwise or crosswise.

Follow-up activities
▲ Carefully cut a pattern or an initial on the flat surface of half a potato before printing with it.
▲ Sort the vegetables according to shape, length, colour or whether they have rough or smooth skins.
▲ Describe the shape or features of a vegetable without showing the children. For example, 'I have a vegetable which is long, flat, thin and green.' Can you guess what it is? (A runner bean.)

Join the conga

Objective
Music – to practise moving together as a group to a particular rhythm.

Group size
Everyone!

What you need
Conga music, a tape recorder if a piano is not available in your room, a large space.

Preparation
Record the conga music and push back any furniture to make the area safe.

What to do
Play the conga music to help the children become familiar with it. Clap out the rhythm with them before you show the steps to match the rhythm. Take five quick steps and on the sixth lift your right leg out to the side. Repeat the steps and lift your left leg out to the side. Now take four slow steps and lift your right leg, and repeat with the left leg.

Line up the children in a queue going from the tallest to the shortest. Ask them to put their hands on the waist of the child in front of them. You join the front of the queue so that the children can copy and follow you weaving in and out around the room. All sing 'la-la-la-la-la-la' to the conga music and lift your legs at the appropriate times. Don't go too fast or the tail of the conga will not be able to keep up! When the children are well practised in dancing the conga, let them take turns to be the leader.

Discussion
How did all the people and animals in the story arrange themselves to pull up the turnip? To get the most pulling power they lined up in a queue, and held onto each other. Are there any times when the children have to queue up? (The supermarket or the bus stop, for example.) Why do people form queues? (It is safer and fairer.)

For younger children
Instead of forming a queue let them dance freely to the conga.

For older children
Encourage older children to count the number of steps they make before they kick. Try varying the speed of the dance.

Follow-up activities
▲ Role-play waiting at a bus stop. What sort of things do people talk about while they are waiting in a queue?
▲ Order a selection of toy animals from the tallest to the shortest.
▲ Let the children arrange themselves in random order and then dance the conga – are there any difficulties?

Join the conga

Arranged by Peter Morrell

Guess what I'm pulling

Objective
PE – to mime different pulling actions.

Group size
Whole group.

What you need
A skipping rope, PE mat, chair, some heavy books, sticking plaster, packet of biscuits with a thread pull for opening, packet of crisps, guitar or string instrument, bicycle pump, sweater.

What to do
Tie the skipping rope onto a chair and then place the books on the chair. With the PE mat behind them in case of falls, let the children take turns at pulling the rope to try to move the books and the chair. They will notice how much effort is needed when pulling something heavy.

Demonstrate other pulling movements: stick the plaster to your skin and ask them to watch your face as you pull it off; show them how to open the packet of biscuits by pulling on the thread; grasp both sides of the crisp packet and pull it open; pull on the strings of the guitar to make a musical sound; show the action of a bicycle pump being used; and finally put on the sweater then pull it off over your head. Ask the children to mime all these pulling actions.

Discussion
In the story how did they pull the enormous turnip out of the ground? (A joint effort.) When do the children use a pulling action? (Getting dressed or pulling open the curtains, for example.) Which animals use a pulling action? (Birds pull worms out of the soil, a dog pulls on a bone, a cat pulls on furniture with its claws, a horse pulls a cart.)

For younger children
Practise pulling off coats.

For older children
Ask the children to take turns to mime the above pulling actions without the 'props' for the other children to guess what's being pulled.

Follow-up activities
▲ Blow up a bicycle tyre or football by pulling and pushing on a pump.
▲ Make crackers by twisting tissue paper at either end round a small construction brick. Pull the cracker open.
▲ Tie two toy vehicles together with some string and let the front one tow the back one.

▲ 18
Starting with story
Traditional story activities

Many hands

Objective
RE – to test out the proverb 'Many hands make light work'.

Group size
Six children.

What you need
Ingredients for making curry (if you do not have the individual spices simply add 1 dessertspoonful of mild curry powder to the softened vegetables): 2 tablespoons of vegetable oil, a selection of vegetables to weigh approximately 750g when prepared (such as turnip, potato, carrot, cauliflower, peas, green and red peppers, spring onions), 1 dessertspoonful each of mustard seeds and cumin seeds, 1 teaspoon each of garam marsala, ground coriander, ground cumin, salt. Three chopping boards, three knives, scissors, a potato peeler, a pan or microwave dish and cover. Access to water and to a cooker.

What to do
Ensure the children have clean hands before handling food. Tell them that you are all going to make a curry – a spicy dish. Let the children wash and prepare the vegetables. Peel and cube the turnips, potatoes and carrot. Cut the spring onions with scissors. Break florets off the cauliflower and slice the peppers. Heat two tablespoons of oil in the pan, add the cumin and mustard seeds, cover and cook for two or three minutes until they have stopped popping. Add the prepared vegetables, remaining spices and a little water. Cook for about 30 minutes (less in a microwave) until the vegetables are soft. Taste and adjust the seasonings before inviting the children to try a little of the curry.

Discussion
The little old man couldn't pull up the enormous turnip on his own. What did he do? He asked for help, lots of help. When everyone pulled the turnip together the many hands made light work. When everyone helped make the curry that also made light work.

For younger children
Boil the turnips, potatoes and carrots and cool them before letting the children chop them.

For older children
Grind the whole coriander and cumin seeds in a pestle and mortar.

Follow-up activities
▲ Leave out the spices from the recipe above to make soup. Add a tin of tomatoes, a vegetable stock cube and more water.
▲ The police use their hands to direct the traffic – see if you can!
▲ Practise other hand customs – shake hands, wave, salute, point, clap, hold hands together.

▲ **19**
Starting with story
Traditional story activities

Lend a hand

How many hands are needed to pull each turnip?

leaves cut from templates

children's own hand outlines

crumpled-up tissue paper pieces

a small turnip

a large turnip

an enormous turnip

Group size
Small groups (to do different parts of the display).

What you need
Blue and black background paper, a small, large and very large piece of card, sharp scissors (for an adult), green and white tissue paper, green activity paper, sheets of different-coloured paper, pencils and scissors for the children, PVA adhesive and spreaders, drawing pins, stapler, labelling card, thick marker pen, a fresh, white turnip, card for templates.

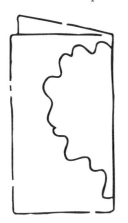

leaf template

Preparation
Draw and cut out the outlines of a small, large and enormous turnip from card. Make different-sized leaf templates to match the sizes of the three turnips. Cut the tissue paper into small squares.

What to do
Give each group of children a different turnip outline. Ask them to crumple up the squares of tissue paper and stick them all over the card outline remembering that a green band goes near the top, as on a real turnip. Fold the green paper in half and help the children to draw round the leaf templates and cut them out. Finally, let them choose a piece of coloured paper to draw their hand outline and cut round it. Assemble the display as shown in the diagram, using drawing pins to arrange it temporarily before stapling it into position.

Discussion
Why are there only two hands round the smallest turnip? (It's easy to pull up.) What do we mean when we say 'lend a hand'? People can help each other out with jobs like the children have all helped to make this display. What sort of things do the children do to help their parents?

Follow-up activities
▲ A car is made of many parts and won't work properly unless all the parts work together. Ask the children to choose a different car part and mime its actions, for example windscreen wipers, steering wheel, indicators, headlights and wheels. Now they can mime all the parts together to get the car working.
▲ Let the children use the crumpled paper technique to cover the outline initial of their name.
▲ Make hand prints to decorate your room.

Under the ground

Group size
Small groups (to do different parts of the display).

What you need
Sheets of black activity paper to cover the display area twice over, brown wrapping paper, fur fabric or brown wool, small pieces of cotton wool, black bin bag, several polystyrene packing chips, lightweight twigs, dead leaves, PVA adhesive and spreaders, craft knife, scissors, stapler, thick green marker pen.

Preparation
Cut some 10cm squares from the bin bag for beetles.

What to do
Ask the children to screw up the large sheets of black paper. Open out this 'soil' to see the creases and texture. Loosely fix one layer of 'soil' to the display area to look bumpy. In the other sheet of 'soil' cut three or four crosses (adults only) and turn back the corners to make holes. Also cut pairs of parallel lines to make slots for worms. Fix this sheet loosely on top of the other to show maximum texture. Show the children

how to tear strips of brown paper and pleat them. Thread these 'worms' through the slots you have cut.

Cut pieces of fur fabric or wool for the back end of rabbits, moles and mice. Stick them into the holes in the black paper. Add white bobtails to the rabbits, and longer wool tails for the mole and mice. Make a broad knot in the bin bag squares and fringe the ends with scissors to look like beetles' legs. Stick the beetles, dead leaves, twigs and polystyrene chippings (pottery) over the display. Draw grass clumps at the top to show the ground above the soil.

Discussion
What is below the ground where turnip roots grow? Can the children name some of the creatures found there? (Worms, beetles, ants, mice, rabbits, moles, voles.) Why do these creatures live underground? (They don't like the light and feel safer.)

Follow-up activities
▲ Draw animals which prefer the dark, such as owls, bats and moths.
▲ Sieve some garden soil through a riddle and see what is left – leaves, twigs, pebbles and other materials found in soil.

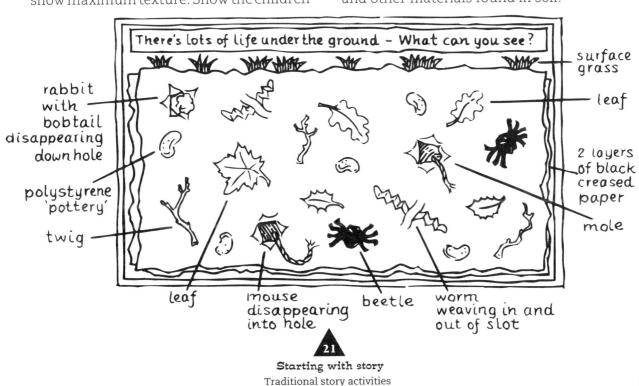

Fill the jacket potato

Group size
Four children.

What you need
750g turnips, four medium-sized potatoes, vegetable oil, salt, butter or margarine. Bowl of warm water and vegetable scrubbing brushes, a pan, fork, knife, four dessertspoons, baking tray, pastry brush, vegetable masher, oven.

Preparation
Peel, slice and boil the turnips until they are soft enough to mash. Drain them and leave them in the pan.

What to do
After they have washed their hands, let the children scrub their potatoes clean. Supervise them while they prick the potato skins with a fork. Place the potatoes on the baking tray and brush them with vegetable oil. Bake them in the oven at 200°C (400°F, Gas Mark 6) for about one hour. Test if they are cooked by piercing them with a knife.

Halve them and allow them to cool sufficiently for the children to be able to scoop the middles out with a spoon. Add the 'middles', salt and a knob of butter to the turnip in the pan. Let the children take turns to mash the potato and turnip together and then fill up their 'jackets' with the mashed mixture. If necessary, pop them back into the oven to heat through before eating them.

Discussion
Although potatoes grow underground they are not a root vegetable but a tuber. What are the little buds on the potatoes called? Each 'eye' on the potato grows a new shoot. What are crisps and chips made from? Some people call potatoes 'spuds'.

Follow-up activities
▲ Try other fillings with the potato such as grated cheese, chopped spring onions, baked beans.
▲ Make a potato creature with cocktail sticks, buttons, bits of wire and a marker pen. Put it in a dark cupboard and it will grow into a funny shape over the next few months. (Be aware that sprouting potatoes are poisonous if eaten.)

chapter two
▶ **introduction** ◀

The Gingerbread Man

This traditional story appeals to children because it is about breaking the rules. The Gingerbread Man doesn't want to be eaten and decides to run away, escaping from more and more people and animals. Finally, he is stopped by the cunning of the fox, whereby hangs the moral of the story – not everyone who is charming can be trusted.

One day a man said to his wife, 'Let's have something tasty to eat!' And so together they made a gingerbread man and put him in the oven to bake. Soon they heard, 'Let me out, let me out!' They opened the oven door and out jumped The Gingerbread Man. 'Stop!' they shouted as they ran after him. But The Gingerbread Man ran on, singing:

'Run, run as fast as you can, you can't catch me, I'm The Gingerbread Man!'

A cow noticed The Gingerbread Man running by and shouted, 'Stop, I want to eat you.' But The Gingerbread Man ran on, singing:

'Run, run as fast as you can, you can't catch me, I'm The Gingerbread Man!'

A horse saw The Gingerbread Man and feeling very hungry shouted 'Stop!' But The Gingerbread Man ran on, singing:

'Run, run as fast as you can, you can't catch me, I'm The Gingerbread Man!'

A schoolboy and girl spotted The Gingerbread Man and shouted 'Stop!' But The Gingerbread Man ran on, singing:

'Run, run as fast as you can, you can't catch me, I'm The Gingerbread Man!'

A dog was startled as The Gingerbread Man ran by, and called 'Stop!' But The Gingerbread Man ran on, singing:

'Run, run as fast as you can, you can't catch me, I'm The Gingerbread Man!'

A cat spied The Gingerbread Man, and was about to pounce when The Gingerbread Man ran on, singing:

'Run, run as fast as you can, you can't catch me, I'm The Gingerbread Man!'

As The Gingerbread Man ran away from the man and his wife, the cow, the horse, the boy, the girl, the dog and the cat, he came to a river. Not wanting to get wet and soggy, he had to stop.

'I'll help you across the river,' said a very polite fox, and tricked The Gingerbread Man into climbing on his tail. As the fox swam across the river, The Gingerbread Man's feet got wet, so he moved to the fox's back, then to its head and finally on to its nose.

The fox threw back his head and snapped his jaws. 'Oh dear!' cried The Gingerbread Man, 'I'm a quarter gone.'

The fox snapped again. 'Oh dear, I'm a half gone!'

The fox snapped yet again. 'Oh dear, I'm three-quarters gone!'

And that was the last thing The Gingerbread Man said, because with the next snap he was all gone.

Starting with story
Traditional story activities

Listen to this!

Objective
English – to listen and match rhyming sounds.

Group size
Six children.

What you need
Photocopiable page 89, a toy van, a toy iron, a small toy pig (sow), a knife (closely supervised), a bottle of sauce, a pan, a 'pearl' necklace, a log, a hat, a box.

Preparation
Enlarge and copy the photocopiable sheet onto card and cut it into individual pictures.

What to do
Ask the children if they can remember who the people and animals were in the story: a man, his wife, a cow, a horse, a boy, a girl, a dog, a cat, a fox and The Gingerbread Man. As they name each one, hold up the card to show them the picture. Now show them the toy van, ask a child to name it and to place it on the picture of the story character which it rhymes with – 'man'. Establish that the iron is a toy and ask them which character rhymes with toy – 'boy'. Show the children each article in turn for them to place on the rhyming character picture – knife with wife; sauce with horse; sow with cow; pearl with girl; log with dog; box with fox; hat with cat; pan with The Gingerbread Man.

Discussion
When words sound the same we say they rhyme. Can the children think whether their own name rhymes with anything? If it is a long name maybe they can shorten it or just rhyme the final syllable. Point out that nursery rhymes are called so because they have rhyming words. Which words rhyme in the nursery rhyme 'Jack and Jill'?

For younger children
Put the article and the picture ready together for them and ask them to say both words, for example 'sauce' and 'horse'.

For older children
Can they name the matching character and article without using the pictures?

Follow-up activities
▲ Give each child a copy of photocopiable page 89 for them to colour and then to overwrite or underwrite the names.

▲ Cut up photocopiable page 89 into pictures, count how many characters there are and put them in order of their appearance in the story.

▲ Together make up some rhymes about the weather or things that you do in your group, for example 'We like to play on a sunny day'.

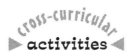

Find the man

Objective
English – to recognise picture clues and use them in a treasure hunt.

Group size
Six children.

What you need
A piece of A5 card, a pencil, scissors, Blu-Tack, a very simple bought jigsaw puzzle.

Preparation
Draw a large outline of The Gingerbread Man onto the piece of card. Cut it into six sections like jigsaw pieces as shown in the diagram. Use these jigsaw pieces to make the treasure hunt clues. On each of the pieces carefully draw a place in your room, indicating where the children will need to look to find the next clue. Clues could be the book rack, a door, the peg pictures, a cupboard, a chair or a radiator, for example.

When the children are not around, fix all the clues in the appropriate places with Blu-Tack. For example, place the first clue on the table – this clue can have the picture of a chair, which is where the next clue can be found.

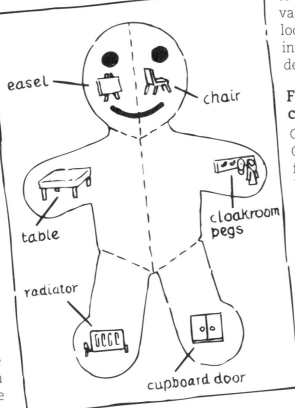

What to do
Ask two children to do the bought jigsaw and show how the pieces fit together. Say that you have hidden six jigsaw pieces which you want them to find and bring back to the group. Explain that on each piece there is a drawing that gives a clue to finding the next jigsaw piece. This is called a treasure hunt.

Tell them the area where they should look for the first picture. When they have found all six pieces, ask them to guess what picture is on the jigsaw and to complete it.

Discussion
How many children could guess what the completed jigsaw would be? Could they understand where to look for the next clue? What other picture clues tell people where to go or what to do? (Road signs, for example.)

A treasure hunt is usually to look for something valuable. Some people look for buried treasure in fields by using a metal detector.

For younger children
Cut the jigsaw of The Gingerbread Man into four pieces only; it will be less for them to find.

For older children
Instead of picture clues, write simple written instructions on the jigsaw pieces.

Follow-up activities
▲ Ask one of the children to hide something and then to direct the others to find it by pointing left or right, under, on top or inside. They should only point, not speak.

▲ Make individual jigsaws using old greetings cards. It is easier if the picture has a heavy black frame drawn round it before being cut out.

▲ Sing the nursery rhyme 'Humpty Dumpty'.

Share the pieces

Objective
Mathematics – to cut shapes into equal parts and to practise sharing.

Group size
Four children.

What you need
20cm squares of white paper, scissors, thick wax crayons.

What to do
Give each child a square of paper and ask them to crayon all over one side, with one colour. Each child's crayon should be a different colour. Show the children how to fold their squares in half by matching corners to corners and creasing with a finger along the folded edge. Ensure that the children understand the words 'corner', 'edge', 'crease' and 'fold'.

Let the children open up the paper and see the two halves. Then fold it back in half again and match the other two corners. Ask them to open up the paper and count the number of small squares – explain that these are called quarters.

Ask them to cut their paper along the creases to separate the quarters and then arrange the cut quarters back into a square again. Each child can now give the other three children in the group one of their quarters to end up with a multicoloured square.

Discussion
The Gingerbread Man cried 'I'm a quarter gone' when the fox snapped at him. Can the children remove a quarter from their own big square? Then The Gingerbread Man cried 'I'm a half gone' – can the children now take away half? What is left? Do they ever cut anything into halves and quarters at home? (Toast, cakes, fruit, for example.)

For younger children
There is no need for them to cut the paper; they can practise folding only, into halves and quarters.

For older children
Show them the ¼ symbol and let them write it onto each of their quarters.

Follow-up activities
▲ Give the children an outline of The Gingerbread Man and ask them to fold and cut it into quarters just like the pieces the fox ate.

▲ Use The Gingerbread Man quarters in a display entitled 'What's he eaten?' (see 'What's inside the fox?', page 36).

▲ Fold a 20cm square of paper into half, then quarters, diagonally. Compare the quartered triangles with the quartered squares.

▲ Cut an apple into quarters and fit the segments back together again with cocktail sticks.

▲ Fold a piece of paper into eighths, count each square and mark it with the ⅛th symbol.

Take a pair

Objective
Mathematics – to find out how many make a pair and to subtract numbers.

Group size
Three children.

What you need
Sheets of A4 paper, pen, tiddlywinks or buttons or small counters, a numbered dice (1 to 6) and shaker, three sticky white labels.

Preparation
Draw an outline of The Gingerbread Man on A4 paper and make a copy for each child. Use the sticky labels to cover the numbers 4, 5 and 6 on the dice. Draw dots on the labels to represent the numbers 1, 2 and 3.

What to do
Give each child The Gingerbread Man outline. Put the counters in the middle of the table. Ask the children how many noses and mouths The Gingerbread Man has, and put one counter on each. How many eyes does he have? Place two counters of the same colour on his eyes. Repeat with his arms and legs, ensuring the counter colours are the same on each pair. Place three counters on his coat buttons.

Then let the children take turns to throw the dice and remove the corresponding counters from the board, for example one for either the mouth or nose, two for a choice of any of the pairs, and three for the buttons. They will have to miss a go if the required number of counters has already been taken. Play on until all the counters have been removed.

Discussion
When you have two the same it is called a pair. Do the children have other pairs? (Eyebrows, knees, shoulders.) What else is described in pairs? (Trousers, scissors, spectacles.) One pair of socks is two and one pair of twins is two children.

For younger children
Ensure that they can identify the numbers and dots on the dice.

For older children
Repeat the game, but this time putting the counters back on The Gingerbread Man.

Follow-up activities
▲ Draw four teeth, ten fingers and toes, and six necklace beads on an A3-sized Gingerbread Man outline, cover them with counters and include numbers 4, 5 and 6 in the dice game.
▲ Stand the children in pairs, one behind the other, and walk round in a 'crocodile'.
▲ Jumble all the children's shoes and put them back into pairs.

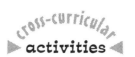

Soggy toast

Objective
Science – to discover that water can change food.

Group size
Six children.

What you need
Three slices of thick white bread, a toaster or means of toasting the bread, one dinner plate, a small jug of water, balance scales.

What to do
Let the children weigh the pieces of bread separately and compare the weights of all three (which should be the same). Toast two pieces of the bread, compare their weight to each other and then to the piece of bread. Notice the changes to the pieces of toast – in how they look, feel and smell. Pour some water onto the plate and place one piece of toast in it. When the toast has absorbed the water, remove it carefully to compare its weight to the unsoaked toast and then to the bread. Notice how the soaked toast has changed.

Discussion
In what way did the bread change when it was toasted? It changed colour and became stiff and crispy. Why did this happen? Did the bread lose most of its moisture? Had its weight changed? When the toast was put into the water what happened to it? When food is in water it soaks some up and then becomes softer. If The Gingerbread Man had tried to swim across the river what would have happened to him?

For younger children
Let them compare crispy to soggy toast (ignore the bread).

For older children
Weigh the bread and toast on graded scales and record the weights in grams.

Follow-up activities
▲ Soak various foods in water and note the changes and how long it takes. Try soaking prunes, sultanas, marrowfat peas, butter beans. Compare the soaked food to some that has not been soaked.
▲ Test different fabrics for absorbency – cotton, plastic, sponge, net.
▲ Leave some orange peel in a warm place to dry out. Examine it and then soak it in water to make it soft again.
▲ Soak some sugar in a glass of warm water. Where has the sugar gone? Leave the sugar water on a glass plate for three or four days to evaporate. Look through a magnifying glass to see what is left in the saucer.

Get me across

Objective
Design and Technology – to design and make models of bridges.

Group size
Whole group then small groups.

What you need
Large sheets of newspaper, cardboard tubes and boxes, large cardboard pieces, sticky tape, stapler, cotton reels, books, building blocks, rulers, a variety of construction toys.

What to do
Talk about crossing a river, and when one of the children mentions bridges tell them that this is what you want them to make. Show them the variety of materials that you have collected and ask them for ideas on how they might be used to make a bridge. Help them by suggesting that the cotton reels, wooden blocks or slices of cardboard tubing might act as pillars to support a book or a piece of cardboard. If a sheet of newspaper is rolled up and secured with sticky tape, it would be stiff enough to bend and hold in a bridge shape. Construction toys can be built into supports for rulers. Let them choose and make their own style of bridge.

Discussion
Why do we need bridges? The Gingerbread Man thought that the fox's back would be a safe way to cross the river. Can the children suggest other ways to cross rivers? (By swimming, by boat, on a ferry, on a hovercraft, by tunnel.) Which of these ways could be used to cross a road or railway line? Have any of the children seen or used a swing-bridge over a canal?

For younger children
Provide the bridge supports and let them choose what they would like to lay across them.

For older children
Encourage them to devise ramps for getting onto the bridge that they have made.

Follow-up activities
▲ Run some toy cars and lorries over the bridge you have made.
▲ Make a bridge out of the furniture and equipment in the room for the children to walk across. A small upturned table supported on blocks could be used.
▲ Sing the nursery rhyme 'London Bridge is Falling Down'.
▲ Move your bodies into differently shaped bridges – curved, flat, sloped.
▲ Read the story of 'The Billy Goats Gruff' who crossed the river.
▲ Practise swimming strokes and pretend you have The Gingerbread Man on your back!

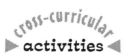

Sugar and spice

Objective
History – to find out how and why spices were used in the past.

Group size
Six children.

What you need
A variety of different strong-smelling items such as powdered and root ginger, a mint-flavoured sweet (or fresh mint leaves), ground cinnamon, cloves, curry powder, orange peel, yeast extract, blackcurrant squash and coffee powder. Enough empty, clean, food containers with lids (for example, a cream carton), a knitting needle or skewer, sticky tape, paper towels.

Preparation
Put a small portion of the strong-smelling item into each container, secure the lid with sticky tape and pierce holes in it. Pour liquids onto a piece of paper towel in the container to avoid spills.

What to do
Ask the children to smell the mint and the root ginger. Do they know what they are? Tell them that they are going to play a smelling game with some other items. Take one item at a time and pass it round for the children to guess what it is. Start with a different child for each new item.

Discussion
The ginger, mint, cinnamon, cloves and curry are either herbs or spices. What are they used for? (For flavouring food and for use in cosmetics, for example.) Before fridges were invented, people couldn't keep their food fresh for very long. They added the strong flavours of herbs and spices to hide the stale taste. Nowadays we use herbs and spices to give us variety. All herbs and spices come from growing plants. Ginger comes from an underground stem, not a root. Root ginger is dried and ground and is used to bake gingerbread men.

For younger children
Let them see what they are smelling – the blackcurrant squash in its bottle, the yeast extract and coffee in their jars and a whole orange.

For older children
Make a class graph of how many children could name the contents of each pot.

Follow-up activities
▲ Make a perfumed greetings card. Draw a picture and rub handcream or body lotion onto different parts of the picture.
▲ Toast some bread, spread it with butter and sprinkle it with cinnamon.
▲ Make a lavender sachet by heaping a spoonful of dried lavender into a small square of muslin or J-cloth. Secure it with an elastic band.

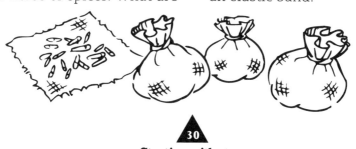

Stop at red

Objective
Geography – to learn about traffic signals and make a set of traffic lights.

Group size
Eight children.

What you need
A chart of basic colours, sheets of white paper, a pencil, ruler, a packet of coloured gummed circles or tissue circles (including red, yellow and green) approximately 76mm in diameter, a cardboard circle of the same diameter for a template, PVA adhesive and spreaders.

Preparation
Prepare a traffic-lights sheet by drawing a large rectangle on a sheet of white paper and then three circles underneath each other within the rectangle. Make a copy for each child. Mix up the colours in the packet of circles.

What to do
Use the colour chart to check that the children know the colours of red, amber (yellowish) and green. (Be aware that some children may be colour blind.) Talk about the function of these three colours when they are used at traffic lights – red means stop, amber is a warning to be careful because the lights are about to change and green means go. Ask the children to pick out a red, yellow and green circle and to stick them in the correct order on a copy of the traffic-lights sheet.

Discussion
The Gingerbread Man kept running away until he was forced to stop. When are the children forced to stop? Traffic lights are one of the safest places to cross the road but the children must never cross without the help of an adult or older child. Where else is it safe to cross the road? (Zebra and pelican crossings.) Everyone should use the Green Cross Code before crossing the road and children must always cross the road with an adult. (Contact your local authority for more information on the Green Cross Code).

For younger children
Tell them the order in which to stick their circles.

For older children
Ask them to write 'stop', 'wait' and 'go' under the appropriate colours on their traffic lights.

Follow-up activities
▲ Let the children run round until you hold up the colour red. They must stop immediately. When you show them the colour amber they should get ready to move, and on green – off they go again.
▲ Make a lollipop sign. Write 'stop' on a circle of card and staple the circle to a lollipop stick.
▲ Draw other traffic signs and learn to recognise them.

Foxy

Objective
Art – to cut out and decorate fox masks.

Group size
Four children.

What you need
Photocopiable page 90, thin card, scissors, a skewer, Plasticine, shirring elastic, a bodkin, brown and black crayons, felt-tipped pens, brown fur fabric or wool or crêpe paper, PVA adhesive and spreaders.

Preparation
Copy the fox mask on photocopiable page 90 onto thin card (enlarging it if necessary), one for each child. Cut out the eye holes on each mask. Pierce through the side marks with the skewer into a lump of Plasticine.

What to do
Help the children to cut round the outline of each fox mask. Ask them to colour it all over in brown and use black for the muzzle (nose and mouth). Let them decorate parts of the mask with fur fabric, wool or crêpe – perhaps the eyebrows and pointed ears.

When the children have finished their masks, thread a piece of elastic through the holes and tie at each end with a knot to hold the masks in place on the children's heads.

Let the children wear the fox masks and encourage them to look at themselves in the cloakroom mirror.

Discussion
A fox has bright eyes and a bushy tail called a 'brush'. A fox is one of the cleverest, most cunning animals. How clever was the fox in 'The Gingerbread Man' story? Foxes live in 'earths' which they make by burrowing into the ground. Their babies are called cubs. Which other animals have cubs? (Lions, tigers, bears.) Foxes are part of the dog family. If someone is foxy it means that they are cunning, sly and may trick you.

For younger children
Cut out the whole mask for them, so that they only need to colour it. If they don't like having a mask on their face they can put their mask on a stick, to be a puppet instead.

For older children
Let them try to cut out the mask eye-holes themselves.

Follow-up activities
▲ Read Aesop's fable about the fox and the crow.
▲ Display a large picture of a fox on a board and give the children a separate wool tail. Blindfold the children, one at a time, and let them try to pin the 'brush' on the fox.
▲ Say the tongue-twister 'Five furry foxes find food fast'.
▲ Read the poem 'The Three Foxes' from AA Milne's book *When We Were Very Young* (Mammoth).

activities

Clap, clap, clap

Objective
Music – to clap out the rhythmical patterns of words.

Group size
Whole group.

What you need
No resources needed.

What to do
Clap once then clap twice and point out that hand clapping can make long or short sounds. Let the children listen and decide whether you are making long or short clapping sounds. When you read the story of 'The Gingerbread Man' to the children, encourage them to join in with the chorus: 'Run, run as fast as you can, you can't catch me, I'm The Gingerbread Man!' R e p e a t the words 'run, run' only, and then clap the two words as you say them. Ask the children to do the same. Now clap the words 'as fast as you can' in the rhythm of the story. Again ask the children to copy you. Add the two phrases together for the children to say and clap with you, 'Run, run as fast as you can'.

Now practise clapping 'you can't catch me' and finally 'I'm The Gingerbread Man'. Eventually put the whole chorus together to be clapped and chanted. Whenever there is a long note in the rhythm tell the children to hold their hands together, waiting for the next beat. Read 'The Gingerbread Man' story again, but this time instead of saying the chorus ask the children to just clap.

Discussion
Can the children think of other ways to copy the rhythm of the words instead of clapping or saying them – tapping their fingers, stamping their feet, singing la-la-la? When they use percussion instruments with music, they are beating in time to the rhythm.

For younger children
Let them clap their hands to 'run, run' only, and say the rest of the chorus.

For older children
Clap any one of the four sections of 'The Gingerbread Man' chorus to the children and see if they can tell which part it is.

Follow-up activities
▲ Beat out the rhythm of 'The Gingerbread Man' chorus using the percussion instruments.
▲ Clap out the rhythm of the forename and surname of each child in turn.
▲ Read the story of 'The Three Little Pigs' and clap to the words 'I'll huff and I'll puff and I'll blow your house down'.

Catch the man

Objective
PE – to play a game of 'Catch The Gingerbread Man'.

Group size
12 children.

What you need
A space for the children to run around (outside or in).

What to do
This game would be better played outside on the grass but if this isn't possible clear your room to allow space for running round.

Ask the children to form a very wide circle with plenty of space between them. Explain that whoever is to be The Gingerbread Man has to run round the circle weaving in and out of the other children. The Gingerbread Man will be chased by another child who can be one of the story characters, who also weaves in and out of the ring of children.

When The Gingerbread Man is caught, the 'catcher' now has a turn at being 'the man', and is chased by one of the other children. If The Gingerbread Man isn't caught after going round the circle twice, let the children pretend that he has now reached the river and can't run away any more. It's time for a new Gingerbread Man!

Discussion
It is much more difficult to run in and out of things than to just run in a straight line. Did any of the children manage to catch the man? In the story, who do the children think would have been able to run the fastest in the chase for The Gingerbread Man? Why couldn't any of the characters catch him? (Any answers could be right!)

For younger children
Let them run round the room anywhere to try to catch The Gingerbread Man.

For older children
Ask them to try running in pairs in and out of the children to try to catch The Gingerbread Man.

Follow-up activities
▲ Animals can also catch. What do spiders catch? (Flies.) What do cats catch? (Birds and mice.) What do birds catch? (Insects and worms.) Suggest what things other animals might catch.

▲ Sing about 'The Old Woman Who Swallowed a Fly'.

▲ Let the children form a circle round you while you throw a large soft ball for each child to catch in turn.

A sliding trick

Objective
RE – to be aware of how easy it is to be tricked.

Group size
The whole group.

What you need
A large piece of stiff paper, a bar or horse-shoe magnet, a paper-clip, the story of the fox and the crow (in *Fables*, edited by Carol Watson (Usborne), for example).

What to do
Read the story of the fox and the crow, which is about a hungry fox who saw a crow with a lump of cheese in its mouth. The fox told the crow how beautiful she was and asked if he could hear her beautiful voice. The crow was so pleased to be asked that she opened her mouth to sing and in doing

so dropped the cheese. The fox ran off with the crow's cheese.

Now fold a piece of stiff paper and hold it with the flap covering your hand. Place the paper-clip on top and using the magnet hidden under the paper, slide the paper-clip around. Ask the children whether a paper-clip can move by itself. Let the children try this trick for themselves.

Discussion
How did the fox trick The Gingerbread Man and how did the other fox trick the crow? The fox tricked The Gingerbread Man by pretending to be helpful; the fox tricked the crow by flattering her. How did you trick the children? Sometimes tricks are just for fun but not always. Children must be careful not to get tricked into going off with

strangers who offer them sweets. Children should never go with people whom they do not know – they might be tricking them.

For younger children
Hold the paper for them while they move the magnet underneath it.

For older children
Draw a 'pathway' on the piece of paper and see if the children can slide the paper-clip along the path by using the magnet.

Follow-up activities
▲ Use the magnet to pull, push and pick up safety pins or paper-clips.
▲ Test what can be moved by a magnet. Try coins, badges, nails, buttons and chalk, for example.
▲ Draw small paper characters from 'The Gingerbread Man' story. Bend their feet and attach a paper-clip to them. Arrange them on a piece of cardboard. Use magnets for the figures to chase The Gingerbread Man.
▲ Play a game where you mustn't answer 'yes' or 'no' to questions. Trick your friend into saying 'yes' or 'no'.

What's inside the fox?

fur or
woollen
ears

pink
backing
paper

doors to
open
to see
inside
fox's tummy

What's the fox eaten?

pieces of
gingerbread
man

fringed
brown paper
strips

fur or
woollen
"brush"

Group size
Six children.

What you need
Pink lining paper, a large piece of brown card, brown wrapping paper, a large white card outline of The Gingerbread Man to fit in the area of the fox's body, brown fur fabric or wool, pencil, ruler, scissors, PVA adhesive and spreaders, a thick black marker pen, two large paper fasteners, brown crayons, Blu-Tack, stapler, labelling card.

Preparation
Draw and cut out a large fox outline on the brown card. Cut two doors in his body which will bend open. Cut out the white card outline of The Gingerbread Man. Cut some brown wrapping paper into strips approximately 30cm long and 8cm wide.

What to do
Show the children how to cut fringes along the strips of brown paper. Overlap and stick these fringes along the body of the fox outline to represent fur. Ensure that you can still open the 'doors'. Colour the fox's

face and stick fur onto his ears. Give him a fur tail. Crayon The Gingerbread Man brown and draw buttons and face features with the black marker pen. Cut him into four large pieces. Line the display area with the pink paper and staple the fox onto it. Insert the paper fasteners as door handles and open the doors. Fix the quarters of The Gingerbread Man inside the fox's tummy using Blu-Tack. Label the display at the top with 'What's the fox eaten?'

Discussion
How many bites of The Gingerbread Man did the fox make? He made four. How many pieces have the children found in his tummy? When the children eat their own gingerbread, how many bites do they take to eat it?

Follow-up activities
▲ Take The Gingerbread Man out of the fox's tummy and reassemble him.
▲ Make more paper gingerbread men, decorate them in different colours and cut each into four pieces. Jumble them up and fix them inside the fox's tummy. Make a game of sorting them all out again.

Our baking

Group size
Ten children.

What you need
Sheets of white A4 paper, black felt-tipped pens, labelling card and a thick black marker pen, all the cooking utensils and ingredients that are needed for making and baking gingerbread men (see page 38), a table and bright cotton tablecloth, coloured lining paper, stapler.

Preparation
Line the display area and place a table in front of it. Make enough 'roof-top' labels to name all the equipment and ingredients.

What to do
Talk through the steps of making the gingerbread men, as described on page 38: (1) weighing the ingredients, (2) heating some of them in the pan, (3) mixing in the dry ingredients, (4) leaving the dough to stiffen, (5) pulling, pushing, rolling and moulding the gingerbread, (6) forming it into a person, (7) adding the currants and mouth, (8) baking the gingerbread in the oven, (9) leaving it to cool, (10) eating it.

Ask each child to draw one of these stages. Staple their drawings to the display area in sequential order, as in a comic strip, and number them clearly. Cover the table with a tablecloth and arrange all the utensils, packets and jars of ingredients. Ask some able children to write the names of all the items on the 'roof-top' labels and position them on the table.

Discussion
When you bake cakes and biscuits you need to follow a recipe. This is a special set of instructions and tells you what ingredients you need and what to do. If you were going to make lemon biscuits what would you need that you didn't use for the gingerbread men?

Follow-up activities
▲ Refer to the numbered pictures on the wall and ask the children what is happening in the picture before number 8, the one after number 3, above picture number 7, under picture number 4, in the first or last picture.
▲ What are spoons used for? (Measuring, stirring, eating, for example.)

Yummy gingerbread men

Group size
Six children.

What you need
50g butter, 100g soft brown sugar, 100g syrup (2 tablespoons), 2 tablespoons of milk, 225g plain flour, 1 level desertspoon of bicarbonate of soda, 1 level teaspoon each of ground ginger and ground cinnamon. A handful of currants and two glacé cherries. Saucepan, scales, mixing spoon, teaspoon, knife (supervised), pastry boards, two greased baking trays, oven, cooling rack, pencil and paper.

Preparation
Let the children watch you prepare the gingerbread. Weigh the ingredients then melt the butter, sugar and syrup gently in the pan, stirring in the sugar (don't let the mixture get too hot). Blend in the milk. Leave this syrup to cool before mixing in the flour and spices and then rest the dough mixture for at least half an hour, or overnight in the fridge.

What to do
Give each child a portion of dough to roll into balls or sausages and then flatten to make into body parts of a gingerbread man. Add currants for eyes, nose and buttons, and a slice of glacé cherry for the mouth. Lift each man carefully onto a greased baking tray (only three men to a tray). It is a good idea to make a paper plan of the baking sheet arrangement showing whose man is whose. Bake them in the oven at 170°C (325°F, Gas Mark 3) for about 20 minutes. They will look soft and puffy, but don't overcook them because they will harden later. Leave them to cool for about five minutes before lifting them onto a wire cooling rack.

Discussion
When you mix certain ingredients together and bake them you can make different kinds of cakes and biscuits. What makes gingerbread taste different from other biscuits? (It is the ginger that gives it its particular taste.) If the children's gingerbread person could get up and run away like the one in the story did, where do they think it would run to?

Follow-up activities
▲ Buy a piece of root ginger from the greengrocer in spring. Chop off a portion and bury it in a pot of soil. Cover the pot with plastic film, keep it warm, damp and light, and in about four weeks you will notice it has begun to sprout. Keep it growing inside.
▲ Drink some ginger ale and see if you can taste the ginger in it.
▲ Make a display of 'Our baking' (see page 37 for ideas).

▶ introduction ◀

Rapunzel

This is a story about wrongdoing and being punished for it. The man had to give up his child because he stole, and the old woman lost Rapunzel because she was jealous and possessive. However, the story ends happily for Rapunzel and the Prince, because traditionally love is more powerful than hatred.

A man and his wife were very excited to be having a baby. One day the wife was feeling tired and fancied eating some lettuce from the neighbour's garden. Her husband crept into the garden on tiptoe, and had gathered a basketful of the lettuce when suddenly the neighbour appeared. She was very angry and would only let him take the lettuce if he promised to give her the new baby. He was so frightened that he agreed.

No sooner was their daughter born than the neighbour, an old woman, came to take her away.

The old woman called the baby Rapunzel and looked after her well. When she grew up she was so beautiful that she wanted to keep her for herself. She locked her in a room at the top of a tall tower, which had no doors or staircase and only one small window.

Whenever the old woman visited she would call, 'Rapunzel, Rapunzel, let down your hair,' and then would climb up the girl's plaits.

Rapunzel was very lonely and spent her time singing, drawing and plaiting her hair. One day a Prince passed by and heard the most beautiful singing. He looked everywhere to discover who was singing and was about to leave when a paper dart landed at his feet. The message on it said 'Hide in the woods till nightfall'.

The Prince hid and watched as the old woman climbed up Rapunzel's hair. When she had gone, he too called, 'Rapunzel, Rapunzel, let down your hair,' and climbed up to meet Rapunzel. They fell in love, and made plans for her escape.

Every time the Prince visited he took a piece of string for Rapunzel to make into a rope-ladder. One day the old woman saw the rope-ladder and found out about the Prince. She was so angry that she cut off Rapunzel's plaits and took her to a place far away.

Next time the Prince came, it was the old woman, not Rapunzel, who let down the hair. He was so frightened that he fell from the plaits onto some sharp rose thorns which pierced his eyes and made him blind.

He wandered blindly through the forest for many years until one day he heard some sweet singing. Rapunzel cried tears of joy to find her Prince again, and when two of her tears splashed onto his eyes he was able to see again. He took her back to his castle, married her and they lived happily ever after.

A flying dart

Objective
English – to fold paper into a dart and write a message on it.

Group size
Six children.

What you need
A sheet of A4 paper and a pencil for each child.

What to do
Show the children how to fold their paper one stage at a time. (1) Fold and crease the paper in half along its length, (2) Open it up again and fold the two top corners into the middle, (3) Fold these corners again into the middle, (4) Fold the folded piece of paper in half again, (5) Fold the square end-flaps back down, (6) Lift these square end-flaps so that each forms a right angle (see diagram). Write a message along one side of the dart, such as 'Hello', 'Goodbye', 'Help!' or anything that the children suggest. Let the children hold the dart at the pointed end from underneath and throw it across the room (being careful of other people's eyes).

Discussion
Rapunzel wanted to explain to the Prince how he could get up the tower to meet her but she didn't want the old woman to hear

her calling out. How did she send a message to the Prince? When you fold paper in a special way you can make it into the shape of a dart. Dart shapes can be directed as they fly through the air. What other ways are there of getting messages to people? (Letters, phone calls, faxes, e-mail.)

For younger children
If they cannot write words let them draw a picture on the side of their dart.

For older children
Write a longer message using both sides of the dart.

Follow-up activities
▲ Make a parachute to fly through the air. Tape four pieces of thread to the corners of a square of tissue paper. Gather the threads and secure them in a blob of Plasticine. Sit on a chair and drop your parachute.
▲ Stand behind a line on the floor with your dart and see how far you can throw it.
▲ Find some sycamore wings from outside and watch how they swirl through the air when you drop them from a height.

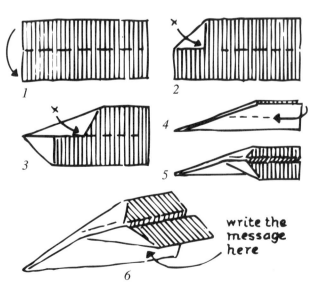

write the
message
here

Find Rapunzel

Objective
English – to become familiar with words of place and position.

Group size
Six children.

What you need
A small doll with long yellow hair – if not available you will need some yellow wool and hairgrips or hairpins, a small set of stepladders.

Preparation
If you need to make suitable hair for the doll, cut the yellow wool into long strands and attach it to the doll's head to look like long golden hair.

What to do
Tell the children to pretend that the doll is Rapunzel who is going to stand in different places and that you want them to tell you where she is. Place the doll under the stepladder, then up at the top, down at the bottom, in front, behind, next to, between the steps. Each time you position the doll ask the children to tell you where she is. When they are familiar with the positions and their words, ask each child in turn to place the doll where you tell them. For example, 'Put Rapunzel in between the first and second step', 'Put Rapunzel in front of the steps'.

Discussion
The Prince couldn't find where the sweet singing voice was coming from. He looked everywhere. Where should he have looked to find Rapunzel? He should have looked up – to the top of the tower. If you look up what can you see – perhaps lampposts, a church steeple, trees, birds, clouds.

For younger children
Limit the positions in which you place the doll to the top or bottom of the steps.

For older children
Include more positions for the doll – against, facing, to the left/right, near/far.

Follow-up activities
▲ Ask the children to cover their eyes while you hide the doll somewhere in the room. Give them position word clues of where to find it.
▲ Play a game of 'Simon says' with the children. For example, 'Simon says sit on your chair, Simon says put your feet under the chair, Simon says sit next to your chair. Sit on the floor.'
▲ Say the action rhyme 'Tall Shop' from *Round and Round the Garden* by Sarah Williams (Oxford University Press).

▲ **41**
Starting with story
Traditional story activities

Plaits and rope-ladders

Objective
Mathematics – to practise counting on while playing a board game.

Group size
Six children.

What you need
Photocopiable page 91, two sheets of A4 card, two dice and shakers, six counters in different colours.

Preparation
Make two card copies of photocopiable page 91 to be the game boards.

What to do
Show the children the game boards and ask them to identify the numbers and the pictures of rope-ladders and plaits. Explain that if you land on a rope-ladder you go down to the square where it ends, and that if you land on a plait you climb up to the square where that starts.

Demonstrate how to play the game by placing a counter on the square marked 'start'. Throw the dice and move the counter the appropriate number of places along the board. For example, if you throw a 4 and land on this rope-ladder it can be ignored because in the game you can only go down a ladder. If you then throw a 1 to move one

place into the square marked number 5 you will climb up the plait to square number 7. The aim of the game is to reach number 20 on the board. Continue to give more examples until you are satisfied that the children can play their own games in groups of three.

Discussion
Rapunzel and the Prince planned to escape by using a rope-ladder. Which other ways could they have come down from the tower – using a parachute, fire-engine ladders, a helicopter, a hot-air balloon? Rapunzel's plaits were used like a rope. What kind of people use ropes for climbing? (Mountaineers, tree surgeons.)

For younger children
Only play to number 10 on the board, and climb up plaits but do not come down rope-ladders.

For older children
Start at number 20 and subtract the numbers shown on the dice to work down to number 1.

Follow-up activities
▲ When the children know numbers beyond 20, let them play the game on a 'Snakes and Ladders' board.
▲ Make a plait using three equal lengths of thick wool tied to a chair-back. Secure the finished plait with an elastic band.

Round and round

Objective
Mathematics – to make a paper spiral staircase and number the steps.

Group size
Four children.

What you need
Stiff paper to make circles (20cm in diameter), scissors, pencils.

Preparation
Cut out a paper circle for each child.

What to do
Ask the children to each point a finger downwards and move it round and round as they lift their arm higher and higher to form the

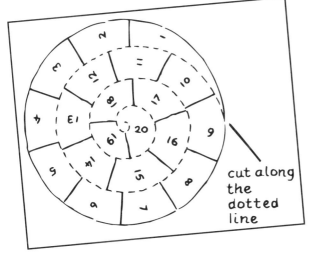

cut along the dotted line

path of a spiral. Explain that they are going to make paper spirals to look like staircases.

Give each child a paper circle and ask them to position their pencil in the centre and make a big dot. Holding the pencil on the dot, they should begin to draw a curve which gets bigger and bigger and stops when it reaches the edge of the circle. Help them to start cutting the pencil marks from the edge of the circle following the markings

until they reach the middle dot. Lines can be then drawn across the spiral shape to represent steps. Ask the children to number as many of the steps as they can (starting from either of the ends).

Discussion
What kind of staircase would fit into a tower? A spiral staircase winds round and round the walls of a tower. Each step has a slanting edge and can be a little awkward to walk up and down. Rapunzel's tower had no staircase so how could anyone get up to her room? Spiral shapes are used in the springs of beds and chairs, and inside the battery compartment of a torch or radio. A helter-skelter at a fairground has a spiral slide running round the outside walls.

For younger children
Give the children ready-cut spirals and ask them to draw the steps and colour them.

For older children
Suggest that they write the number words on each step – first, second, third, fourth and so on.

Follow-up activities
▲ Wind a piece of florist's wire round a thick pen to form a spiral shape and compare it to the thread on a screw.
▲ Open a retractable ball-point pen and find the spring. Will the pen retract without the spring?
▲ Pretend to walk up and down a spiral staircase – does it make you dizzy?

Plaited bread

Objective
Science – to observe the action of yeast and make a plaited loaf.

Group size
The recipe makes enough dough for 12 children.

What you need
A small bowl with 60ml warm water, 2 level teaspoons of dried active baking yeast, 1 teaspoon of sugar, 60g margarine, 225ml of boiling water, 1 level teaspoon of salt, 100g sugar, two medium-sized eggs (beaten), 750g strong white bread flour, beaten egg and sesame seeds for glazing. Fork, two teaspoons, dessertspoon, bowl scraper, large bowls, tea towel, pastry board, two greased baking trays, pastry brush, oven.

Preparation
Stir the yeast and one teaspoon of sugar into the warm water, and leave it for about 15 minutes until it froths and has doubled in size. Show this to the children.

Pour the boiling water over the margarine (away from the children) and stir until it has melted, then add the salt and rest of the sugar. When it's cool, add the beaten eggs and the frothed yeast mixture. Add the flour gradually and knead it for about ten minutes until it is smooth and springy. Place it in a greased bowl, grease the top (to prevent the towel sticking), and cover it with a tea towel. Leave the dough to rise in a warm place until it has doubled in size.

What to do
Give each child 100g of the risen dough (after they have washed their hands). Show them how to roll it into a long snake between both hands held up in the air. Help them to divide the 'snake' into three equal pieces, lay them flat and plait them into a little loaf. Leave them on a baking tray for a further hour, brush with beaten egg-mix and sprinkle with sesame seeds. Bake in the oven at 190°C (375°F, Gas Mark 5) for about 20 minutes.

Discussion
Yeast is alive and will grow when it is warm and fed with sugar. It puts the air bubbles into bread. Rapunzel plaited her long hair just like the children have plaited the bread. This bread is called Challah and is made each week to celebrate the Jewish sabbath.

For younger children
Make one large loaf for them to plait.

For older children
Let them help to make the dough.

Follow-up activities
▲ Make a large loaf by plaiting four lengths.
▲ Roll dough lengths of 20cm and tie a knot in each piece of dough to make some individual rolls.

A knotty problem

Objective
Design and Technology – to tie knots and create a rope-ladder.

Group size
Four children.

What you need
A ball of string (thick string is easier for young children to handle), scissors, a 50cm measure.

Preparation
Cut the string into at least twenty pieces 50cm long.

What to do
Give the children five pieces of string each and ask them to think of ways that they can use them to make their own rope-ladder. Hopefully someone will suggest knotting the pieces together. Make sure that the children know how to tie a knot, first using only one piece of string and then tying two end-pieces together. Eventually they may discover that they can link the lengths of string, tying the ends of each link together in a knot, to form a rope chain which could be used for a 'rope-ladder'.

Discussion
The Prince took pieces of rope to Rapunzel each time he visited her so that she could make a ladder. Why did she need a rope-ladder? It would have been impossible to escape down her own hair! Rope and string are made by twisting together the tough fibres of growing plants such as cotton, hemp or straw. Today rope is often made from man-made materials such as nylon.

For younger children
Use one piece of string only and tie simple knots along its length.

For older children
Link all the individual rope-ladders together, estimate how far their length will reach across the room and then check your estimate.

Follow-up activities
▲ Unravel a piece of string and see how many strands you can count.
▲ Weave pieces of string in and out of a fallen tree branch.
▲ 'Turn' a skipping rope and see how many times you can skip before you trip on the rope.
▲ What kind of people use ladders in their work? (Window-cleaners, builders, fire-fighters, for example.)
▲ Thread thin string through a large-eyed, blunt needle. Sew some loosely woven fabric and see how important it is to knot the string first.

Powdered wigs

Objective
History – to find out about wigs and to role-play hairdressers.

Group size
Eight children.

What you need
A wig, tin of baby powder, two or three combs, jug of water with diluted disinfectant, a packet of hair-clips, dustpan and brush, shallow washing-up bowl, clean old bath towel, two worn clean men's shirts on coat hangers, scissors, empty shampoo and conditioner bottles, two cardboard tubes from kitchen towels, two mirrors (preferably on stands), chairs and tables, play money in a till, a toy telephone, notebook and pencil.

Preparation
Cut off half of the shirt collars and sleeves for overalls. Cut the towel up to make small towels. Bend and crease the cardboard tubes in half to use as hair-dryers.

What to do
Wear the wig, powder it and talk about its history (see Discussion). Help the children set up a hairdressing salon. Make a reception area – hang up the overalls, place the cash till, telephone, notebook and pencil for booking appointments on a table with a chair behind. For the backwash put the bowl on a table with a chair in front of it. Arrange a pile of folded towels and the shampoo and conditioner bottles. In the styling area put mirrors on two tables with chairs facing them and the dustpan and brush underneath. Lay out the hair-clips, hair-dryers and put combs in the diluted disinfectant. Show the children how to move their fingers in a scissor-like action for pretend hair cutting. Ensure that they put the combs into the diluted disinfectant before using them on each other's hair.

Discussion
How did Rapunzel wear her hair? In times past it was fashionable to wear wigs which were made out of people's hair. Children were not allowed to go out on their own in case their hair was cut off by a thief for wig-making. Another custom was to whiten hair, but they used flour instead of baby powder. Sometimes insects and mice would get in their hair to eat the flour!

For younger children
They can be in charge of folding the towels and keeping them in a tidy pile.

For older children
Let them write down the 'client's' names in the appointments diary.

Follow-up activities
▲ Make a display of 'Our hairstyles' (see page 53).
▲ Blindfold a child and see if he or she can tell who other children are just by feeling their hair.

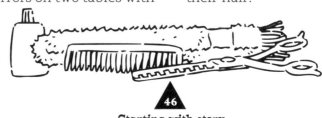

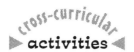

Above the world

Objective
Geography – to appreciate that things look different when viewed from above.

Group size
Four children.

What you need
A deep box full of dry sand, an eggcup, drinking glass, pencil, cardboard tube, ruler, tin of baby powder, a piece of A3 green card, pieces of green and brown fabric and different textured paper in the same shades, scissors, PVA adhesive and spreaders, thick black marker pen.

Preparation
When the children are not around, bury the eggcup, glass, pencil, cardboard tube, ruler and baby powder in the sand so that only the top of each object shows.

What to do
Can the children recognise and name the articles that have been buried in the sand? Point out that things look very different when viewed from above.

Explain that they are going to make a picture of what Rapunzel might have seen from her window in the tall tower. Cut out irregular pieces of paper and fabric and glue them onto the green card as if they were different fields next to each other. Overlap some field edges so that the card doesn't show through.

Finally, draw in some hedge lines with the black marker pen.

Discussion
Were the children able to identify from above the things buried in the sand? If you stand on the ground in a field you can see it all around you. What would you see if you looked at the same field from above? A field in the countryside would have lots of other fields around it. Rapunzel lived in a tall tower and would have been able to look down on a giant patchwork quilt of fields.

For younger children
Cut out the irregular pieces of paper and fabric ready for them to glue onto the card.

For older children
Ask the children to make individual patchwork fields for the display 'A tall tower' on page 52.

Follow-up activities
▲ Bury a toothbrush, toothpaste and some other articles up to their tops in the sand – can the children guess what they are?

▲ Place a doll's house in the middle of a table and ask the children to sit around it. Can they describe what they can each see? Everyone can see different things.

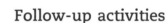

Patterned notes

Objective
Art – to practise the skill of cutting out and to create a pattern.

Group size
Six children.

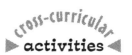

What you need
An example of sheet music showing musical notes, sheets of black paper, sheets of white A4 paper, white crayons or white chalk, scissors, glue sticks or PVA adhesive and spreaders.

What to do
Show the children the sheet music, with notes printed on each stave. Point out that some of the notes have their 'heads' at the top of 'tails' and some have their heads at the bottom of 'sticks' – just like some of the letters of the alphabet.

Give each child a piece of black paper, white paper, a white crayon and scissors. Ask them to draw a letter 'b' on the black paper with a thick 'stick' and 'tail', big enough to be cut out. When they have cut out several, show them how the letters can be turned over to form the shape of musical notes. Arrange them in a pattern on the white paper and then stick the 'heads' of the notes down. Leave the sticks and tails unstuck and bent forward slightly to give depth to the picture.

Discussion
Music is written down by using musical signs called notes. Letters are signs that are used to write down words. Musical notes need to be written on five parallel lines called the stave. When Rapunzel was locked up in her tower room it was very dull and miserable. She loved singing and music and so decided to make a musical note pattern to brighten up the walls. In what other ways can rooms be brightened up? (Pictures, plants, books, lamps.)

For younger children
Cut out the notes ready for them to stick onto paper to make their own pattern.

For older children
Let them draw a large stave and stick the notes onto it like real music.

Follow-up activities
▲ Join several stave patterns together to make a frieze for the room.
▲ Draw and cut out some other musical symbols to add to the pattern – base and treble clefs, sharps and flats.
▲ Cut out large notes and hang them from a coat-hanger to make a mobile.

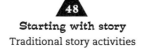

Sweet singing

Objective
Music – to sing and play a guessing game.

Group size
12 children.

What you need
A handkerchief or small scarf.

What to do
Tell the children that they are going to play a singing game and they will need to learn the following words to sing to the tune of 'The wheels on the bus':

> The Prince heard a voice he didn't know,
>   didn't know, didn't know,
> The Prince heard a voice he didn't know,
>   Whose was the voice he heard?

Pick one child to be the Prince then help the other children to sit down in a circle on the floor. Give the handkerchief to the Prince and ask him or her to run round the outside of the circle while everybody sings the song. When you get to the last word of the song 'heard', the Prince drops the handkerchief behind the child he or she is passing. This child now stands up and runs round the outside of the circle in the opposite direction to the Prince. The aim is to see who can get back first to sit down in the empty space. The loser becomes the next Prince.

Discussion
When the Prince heard Rapunzel singing he didn't know who it was. Can you tell who a person is from his or her singing voice? Some people sing with very deep voices and some with very high voices. What is a group of people called who sing together? (A choir.) Which animals can sing? Garden birds sing a lot especially in the early morning – it is called the dawn chorus.

For younger children
Invite the child with the handkerchief to hold hands with the Prince and to walk round the circle together, then back to their places.

For older children
Ask them to run round the circle twice before they sit down in the empty space.

Follow-up activities
▲ Practise singing the nursery rhyme 'Three Blind Mice', and then see if you can sing it in the round. Try to do the same with the song 'London's Burning'.
▲ Record the children's voices individually on a tape recorder. Play the tape back to them and see if they can tell which is their own voice.
▲ Which are their favourite 'pop' songs – can they sing them?

Neighbour's footsteps

Objective
PE – to practise walking on tiptoe while playing a game.

Group size
Whole group.

What you need
A felt-tipped pen and a pencil.

What to do
Hold up the pointed end of the pencil to see if the children know that it is called the 'tip'. Similarly, find out if they know why a felt-tipped pen is so called. Ask them to walk round the room and listen to the noise their feet make. Show the children how to stand on tiptoe and ask them to walk round the room like this.

Explain how to play the game 'Neighbour's footsteps'. The children should stand at one end of the room while you face the wall at the other end. Tell them to pretend that they have just climbed into the neighbour's garden, like the husband in the story. They are to creep towards you and the 'lettuce' without you seeing them move. Whenever you look round they have to 'freeze' into statues. If you see them actually moving, they have to go back to the beginning again. The aim is to be able touch the wall where you are standing without being seen to move.

Discussion
The tip of something is the very end of it and it is usually pointed. How do you walk when you want to be very, very quiet? What part of your foot is off the ground when you walk on tiptoe? (Your heel.) In the story why did the husband walk on tiptoe in the neighbour's garden? (To be very quiet.)

For younger children
They don't need to go back to the beginning until the second time you see them moving.

For older children
When one of them reaches the neighbour's wall they can take their turn to be the neighbour.

Follow-up activities
▲ Suggest all the types of people who might walk on tiptoe and why – a sleeping baby's mother, latecomers to a concert, a ballet dancer to be graceful, small children who can't reach the light switch, grown-ups going through puddles!

▲ Freeze a balloon full of water then peel off the rubber and float the ice balloon in a bucket of water. You will only be able to see the top of it like the 'tip' of an iceberg.

▲ 50
Starting with story
Traditional story activities

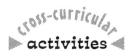
A dotty alphabet

Objective
RE – to appreciate the usefulness of the Braille alphabet.

Group size
Eight children.

What you need
A pegboard and pegs, alphabet chart, photocopiable page 92 and a pencil for each child. A few pieces of carpet tiles or offcuts (unnecessary if your room is carpeted), blindfold.

What to do
Point to a letter on the alphabet chart for a child to name. Ask the children to shut their eyes and see if they can tell which letter you are pointing at now. Mark out the letter 'A' with pegs on the pegboard and invite the children to feel it. Blindfold a willing child, mark out another letter on the pegboard and see if he or she can feel what it is. Repeat the process with other children and other letters.

Give each child a copy of the Braille alphabet on photocopiable page 92 and point out the dots and letters. Place each sheet on a piece of carpet and ask the children to carefully prick right through each dot with a pencil. Then turn the sheets over and let them feel the dots for each letter with their eyes shut.

Discussion
When the rose thorns pierced the Prince's eyes he was blinded. At the age of three, Louis Braille went into his father's saddle workshop and tried to cut some leather with a sharp knife. The knife slipped and went into his eye and he was blinded. At a special school for the blind he learned to read by touching large raised alphabet letters. It was very slow, so when he grew older he invented a much quicker system. This used only six raised dots arranged in different ways. Why do you find the Braille alphabet in herb gardens and on bleach bottles? Why are there bumpy paving stones at pedestrian crossings?

For younger children
Prick through only those dots that represent the alphabet letters they know.

For older children
Ask the children to write their own names in Braille dots.

Follow-up activities
▲ Ask one child to shut his or her eyes and hold onto the shoulders of another child whose eyes are open and who can guide the 'blind' child round the room.
▲ Contact the Guide Dogs for the Blind Association and ask for information about guide-dogs.
▲ Use tiny Plasticine or Blu-Tack balls to make a dice suitable for a blind person.

▲ 51
Starting with story
Traditional story activities

A tall tower

Group size
Six children.

What you need
A piece of grey plastic pipe – size 11cm diameter and approximately 40cm tall (ask a friendly plumber), a sheet of thick grey A3 paper, a large dinner plate (28cm diameter), pencil, scissors, stapler, two indelible black marker pens, sticky tape, a small piece of yellow card, a long woollen plait (see follow-up activities to 'Plaits and rope-ladders', page 42), patchwork fields (see 'Above the world', page 47), four long wooden building blocks, labelling card.

What to do
Share the jobs fairly between the children to ensure that they are all involved in making the tower. Make a cone shape by drawing round a dinner plate onto a sheet of A3 paper, cut round the circle and cut one straight line into the middle, wrap the circle round into a cone shape and secure. Draw roof tiles onto the cone with a marker pen and secure it to the pipe tower with sticky tape. Draw builders'

brick patterns onto the pipe tower. Near the top of the tower stick the yellow card as a small window, mark the window panes and 'hang' the plait from the window. Arrange the patchwork fields across the table top and place the tower in the middle of the fields, stabilising it with the four building blocks. Label the display 'Rapunzel's tower'.

Discussion
A tower is a tall, square or circular building and is usually part of another building. In the past, towers were built tall for defence reasons and to enable them to be used as observation posts. Why was Rapunzel put in the tower? (So nobody could reach her.) Which tower pictures have the children seen? (They may have seen Blackpool Tower, the Post Office Tower in London, the Eiffel Tower in Paris or the Leaning Tower of Pisa.)

Follow-up activities
▲ Each day, alter the length of the plait and the height of the tower (stand it on bricks). Add labels – 'How long is Rapunzel's plait today?' and 'How tall is the tower today?'
▲ Place some toy farm animals and buildings in the display fields.
▲ Build a square tower with the construction toys – don't forget the window.

cut here to make cone for the roof

patchwork fields

bricks & tiles drawn on with marker pen

Rapunzel's plaited hair

stabilising wooden blocks

Rapunzel's tower

Our hairstyles

Group size
Four children at a time.

What you need
Display board, background frieze paper, one piece of A4 card for each child, PVA adhesive and spreaders, scissors, pencils, crayons and felt-tipped pens, stapler, labelling card and marker pen, a mirror on a stand. An assortment of different textured materials such as string, raffia, unravelled knitted wool and some new knitting wool, curly pasta, macaroni, vermicelli, wood curls, crêpe paper, paper for pleating and fringing, fluted pastry cases, corrugated cardboard, bubblewrap, sandpaper, boxes, plates.

Preparation
Pleat one piece of paper and fringe another to use as examples. Unravel some knitted wool. Lay out all the materials so that they are easy for the children to see. Line the display board with frieze paper and write a label with each child's name on it (they may be able to do this for themselves).

What to do
Explain that you are planning to display all their different hairstyles. Ask the children in the group to sit in front of the mirror one at a time, to look at their hair. Give them each a piece of card and tell them to make a big drawing of their face. Let them choose one of the materials that is most like their hair texture. (It doesn't matter if this isn't accurate!) If they choose the pleated or fringed paper encourage them to make their own. Then they can stick the 'hair' in place on their drawing. Staple all their pictures onto the display area and label it 'Our hairstyles'. For the time being, do not label each picture.

Discussion
People have different hair colour and texture. Can the children name hair colours (blonde, red, black, brown, grey, white) and hair textures (straight, wavy, curly, wiry, permed)? What does being bald mean?

Follow-up activities
▲ Ask the group to guess whose picture is whose from the hairstyles. Tell the children to keep quiet if it is their own picture. Then staple each child's name to his or her picture.
▲ Let the children measure the length of the longest part of their friend's hair. Write the measurement up on their name label.

Salad faces

Group size
Six children.

What you need
Lettuce (if possible, a curly leafed type), a selection of the following: cherry and large tomatoes, two eggs, a small cucumber or gherkins, carrots, mustard and cress, watercress, bean sprouts, spring onions or chives, fresh parsley, coriander and fennel foliage, black olives or currants. A small sharp knife, a potato peeler, a pair of kitchen scissors, a grater, a colander, a chopping board, a washing bowl and source of water, paper towels, a dinner plate (or a paper plate) for each child.

Preparation
Hard boil, peel and slice the eggs.

What to do
First ensure the children wash their hands before handling food. Share out the following tasks: wash all the salad ingredients, drain them through the colander and pat dry with the paper towels; halve some of the cherry tomatoes (closely supervise the knife); slice the cucumber thinly; grate some of the carrot.

Give the children one plate each and ask them to choose some of the ingredients to make a salad face. Suggest that hair can be made with torn lettuce leaves, parsley, fennel or coriander, eyes can be slices of egg or cucumber with an olive or currant, eyebrows can be grated carrot, cress, bean sprouts or chives, cheeks can be half tomatoes and mouths can be strips of tomato or carrot. When they have finished their salad faces they can eat them!

Discussion
In the story the wife saw the fresh lettuce growing over the wall and thought it would taste delicious. Which salad vegetables do the children think are delicious? If the salad vegetables were cooked would they still be crispy? Many vegetables can be eaten raw and are very good for you.

Follow-up activities
▲ Use more salad vegetables to add extra features to your salad face, such as spring onion bulb earrings, a chive hair bow, a carrot bow-tie, a bean sprout moustache or beard.

▲ Make a display of different shapes and colours of lettuce.

▲ Use toothpicks or cocktail sticks to pin the salad pieces onto a whole potato, carrot, apple or orange to make vegetable creatures.

▲ Cut cabbage leaves with scissors, grate some carrot and then mix with salad cream to make coleslaw.

cress eyebrow

egg-slice eye with an olive

tomato nose and cheek

lettuce hair

spring onion earring

carrot mouth

bean-sprout beard

chapter four

Hansel and Gretel

Hansel and Gretel is a classic story of how good triumphs over evil. The two young children first manage to outwit their cruel stepmother, then the wicked woman and finally they find safety in the arms of their loving father.

A poor woodcutter lived with his family at the edge of a forest. They were often short of food, and one evening the children, Hansel and Gretel, overheard their stepmother persuading their father to get rid of them. Hansel and Gretel were very upset, but they made a plan and crept out to collect some pebbles from the garden.

Next day, as the family walked into the forest, Hansel secretly dropped the pebbles from his pocket, one at a time. Soon their stepmother said, 'You children rest here while your father and I go to cut some wood. We'll be back soon.'

But by dark they still hadn't returned. Fortunately, the children could follow the trail of their dropped pebbles which shone in the full moon like little white snowballs.

When they arrived home, their father was overjoyed, but their stepmother was not – she looked furious.

Shortly, they again heard their stepmother planning to get rid of them. They wanted to collect more pebbles but she had locked their bedroom door.

Next morning, their stepmother gave Hansel and Gretel a piece of bread each. Secretly they dropped crumbs of bread along the way. When they reached the middle of the forest, their father made them a fire before he and their stepmother left. They did not return, so the children looked for the breadcrumbs to follow. But the birds hadn't left a single crumb! Hansel and Gretel were terribly frightened and tried to remember which trees they had passed, but there was not enough light from the new moon to see.

They wandered round and round in the forest, completely lost until they stumbled upon a candy house made of sweets, biscuits and chocolates. They were so hungry that they helped themselves to pieces of house!

A woman came out of the candy house and invited them in for pancakes and a drink. But she was not a good woman. She locked Hansel up for a week to fatten him and then told Gretel to light the oven. The woman opened the oven door to test the heat and Gretel pushed her into the oven and slammed the door. Gretel rushed to free Hansel, they grabbed some jewellery and ran through the forest right into the arms of their father, who was trying to find them. When they reached home, they found that their stepmother had left in a fit of rage, and the three of them lived very happily without her!

Pocket treasures

Objective
English – to play a memory game to improve reading skills.

Group size
Six children.

What you need
An eraser, small pencil, elastic band, coin, comb, paper handkerchief, paper-clip, a bunch of keys, LEGO brick, a piece of jigsaw puzzle, photograph, a tray and something to cover it, such as a tea towel.

Preparation
Put all the items except the tray and towel into your pockets (if necessary, wear a jacket).

What to do
Ask each of the children if they have anything in their pockets, and if they would mind showing the contents to the rest of the group. Ask them to tell you what they think you are carrying in your pockets. Proceed to show them each item in turn, inviting them to name it. Repeat the name back to them to ensure that each child has heard it.

Place all the items on the tray for the children to take a good long look. Tell them you would like them to try to remember all the things before you cover them up with the tea towel. See how many of the items the children can remember that are on the covered tray.

Discussion
What did Hansel and Gretel have in their pockets the first time they went into the forest? (Pebbles.) Why do people carry things in their pockets? Do they carry things in their pockets that they use often? Perhaps you carry a special object in your pocket that you like very much. People sometimes put things in their pockets when they are tidying up. Why is a particular type of money called 'pocket money'? Which animal has a pocket or pouch for its baby? (A kangaroo.)

For younger children
Restrict the contents of your pocket to three or four items only.

For older children
Ask them to write a list of everything that was on the tray, or to draw the items.

Follow-up activities
▲ Make a collection of items that different people would carry in their pockets and let the children guess who would carry what, for example a screwdriver, stethoscope, torch, piece of pipe, secateurs, lipstick, toy car.

▲ Only fairly small items will fit in pockets. Let the children see how many small toys they can fit in their pockets. Make sure that all the toys are returned to the right place!

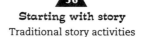

Initial blocks

Objective
English – to recognise personal initials and hammer them into a block.

Group size
Four children.

What you need
Pencils and some practice paper, five rectangular pieces of softwood – size approximately 10cm x 15cm (balsa is particularly suitable and pine offcuts can sometimes be obtained from builder's merchants), sandpaper, a packet of steel tacks (2cm), five small hammers (not toys), Blu-Tack or Plasticine, a thick pencil.

Preparation
Sandpaper the blocks of wood until they are smooth enough for the children to handle. They may be able to do this for themselves.

What to do
Ask the children to write their first name on some practice paper. Make sure that they use a capital letter at the beginning. Explain that this first letter is their initial and that you want them to write it on the block of wood you are going to give them, writing the letter as large as they can to fill the space.

After each child has written their initial on their block, let them take it in turns to practise hammering tacks into your piece of wood, under close supervision. For extra safety, a blob of Blu-Tack can be used to hold the tack in place. When they have practised sufficiently, let them hammer tacks along the outline of their initial on their own block of wood. There is no need for them to hammer the tacks right in.

Discussion
Hansel and Gretel's father was a woodcutter who cut down trees for people to use in different ways. What kind of things are made from wood? (Paper, furniture, pencils, bird-tables, sheds, fences.) Woodcutters are sometimes called tree-surgeons because they look after trees to make sure they are safe. Why do people use their initials? Do you think it is because their initials take up less room than their full name?

For younger children
Write their initial for them onto the wood, so that they have an outline to follow.

For older children
Ask the children to use the initials from their first name and surname to outline with tacks on the wood.

Follow-up activities
▲ Write up all the children's initials to see if they can recognise to whom they belong.
▲ Initials are used all around us – what does TV mean, and what does 'M' on a traffic sign refer to? (Motorway.) What other initials can the children suggest?
▲ Try screwing a screw into wood using a screwdriver then compare screws with nails and tacks.

Fatten him up

Objective
Mathematics – to recognise that each week has seven days.

Group size
Seven children.

What you need
Food advertisements from newspapers, magazines or supermarkets, sheets of white A4 paper, a strip of card (800cm x 100cm), pencil, ruler, thick marker pen, scissors, PVA adhesive and spreaders, sticky tape.

Preparation
Write out the days of the week across the cardboard strip. Cut the pieces of A4 paper in half lengthwise to make seven strips, and write a different day at the top of each strip.

What to do
Ask the children what day it is today and how many days there are in a week. Say the days of the week with them as you point out the words on your chart, and then give each child a strip of paper headed by a day.

Show the children the food advertisements and ask them to name the foods shown and to cut out what they think

Hansel might have eaten on one of the days that he was locked up. Let them stick the foods onto the paper strips, then match and stick each day's menu strip to the week chart. How many menus are there?

Monday	Tuesday	Wednesday	Thursday	Friday	Saturday	Sunday

Discussion
Why did the woman want to fatten up Hansel? Would there be more of him to eat? Some foods would have made Hansel fat more quickly than other types of food. Sweets, sugary drinks, crisps, chocolates and cakes are more fattening foods. If he had eaten lots of fresh fruit and vegetables, yogurt, cheese and milk he would have had lots of energy without getting too fat. Hansel was locked up for a week – how many days would he have been there if he had been locked up for two weeks?

For younger children
If they are not yet very good at cutting, help them to tear the foods from the advertisement sheets.

For older children
Divide their menu strip into three areas for breakfast, lunch and supper and ask them to stick foods into the appropriate sections.

Follow-up activities
▲ Draw foods on a menu strip instead of cutting and sticking.
▲ Make up a day's menu for a cat, a dog or a garden bird.
▲ Say the rhyme 'Monday's child is fair of face' from *The Oxford Nursery Rhyme Book* compiled by Iona and Peter Opie (Oxford University Press).

Starting with story
Traditional story activities

Shapes at night

Objective
Mathematics – to recognise, name and crayon the different shapes of the moon.

Group size
Six children.

What you need
A piece of thick A4 card, a craft knife, a mug, sheets of black A4 paper, white or silver crayons for each child, paper-clips.

Preparation
Draw round the base of the mug to make a circle, half-circle and crescent shape on three of the quarters of the thick card. Cut out the shapes with a craft knife to make a moon-phase stencil.

What to do
Point to the full moon on the stencil and ask the children what shape it is (a circle), then ask what shape the half moon is (half-circle or semicircle), and finally the new moon (a crescent shape). Secure the stencil over a piece of black paper with some paper-clips, and let a child draw the moon outlines with a white or silver crayon. When the outlines have been drawn, pass the stencil to the next child and so on. Once drawn, the outlines can be filled in. Point out that the final quarter of paper has no moon showing at all.

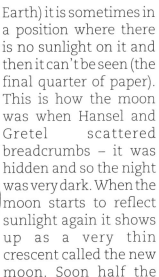

Earth) it is sometimes in a position where there is no sunlight on it and then it can't be seen (the final quarter of paper). This is how the moon was when Hansel and Gretel scattered breadcrumbs – it was hidden and so the night was very dark. When the moon starts to reflect sunlight again it shows up as a very thin crescent called the new moon. Soon half the moon is lit up and then the whole moon is shining. This is called a full moon.

For younger children
Draw the outlines of the moons for them.

For older children
Ask them to write 'new moon', 'half moon' and 'full moon' under the appropriate shapes.

Follow-up activities
▲ Compare a marble to a tennis ball to show the difference in size between the moon and the Earth. Which is bigger? (The Earth.)
▲ Sing and dance 'Sally go round the moon' from *My Very First Mother Goose* by Iona Opie (Walker Books).

Discussion
The moon does not have its own light so what makes it shine? (The light from the sun.) As the moon moves round (the

Leafy clues

Objective
Science – to examine and sort leaves.

Group size
Six children.

What you need
Six different leaf varieties such as laurel, oak, Scots pine, birch, beech, sycamore, horse chestnut, lilac, ornamental cherry, ivy.

What to do
Let the children handle the leaves and compare the sizes and shapes. Point out the leaf edging and show them how to hold them up to see whether any light shows through. Let them feel the texture and thickness of the leaves and also smell them. Mix all the leaves together and ask the children to sort them out into sets. When they have finished ask them to explain how they have sorted them – was it by thickness, shape, size, leaf edge?

Discussion
When Hansel and Gretel were left in the wood they tried to find their way out by remembering the leaves of the trees they had passed, but it was dark and they couldn't see. What differences did the children notice in the leaves? The shapes vary; some are hand-shaped, some are long and some narrow or spiky. The edges also vary; some are straight, some are jagged like teeth, some are wavy

and some have lobed edges like the children's earlobes. Were all the leaves the same thickness? Thicker leathery leaves like laurel, holly and ivy are evergreen and do not fall off the trees in autumn like the thinner types of leaves (birch, beech, sycamore).

For younger children
Let them sort two varieties of leaves only.

For older children
Ask them to select the leaves that you ask for – thick, thin, jagged-edged, wavy-edged.

Follow-up activities
▲ Ring the odd one out and finish the pictures on photocopiable page 93.
▲ Staple different types of leaves to a piece of paper and draw round the edges. Remove the leaves and see the outline.
▲ Collect and sort other things which come from trees such as conkers, acorns, ash-keys and fir-cones.
▲ Fasten a thick leaf, vein side up, to a piece of paper with a paper-clip. With paper uppermost, rub a wax crayon lengthways until the impression of the leaf shows.
▲ Place a thin leaf on a paper towel. Hold it at on end with a finger while tapping the leaf repeatedly with the bristles of a nailbrush. The flesh of the leaf disappears leaving a skeleton of ribs and veins.

Beads and bracelets

Objective
Design and Technology – to design and make jewellery from sawdust dough.

Group size
Six children.

What you need
A small block of wood and piece of sandpaper, five mugs of fine sawdust (can be bought medicated in bags from a pet shop), one generous mug of dry wallpaper paste (no fungicide), four cups of water, a large mixing bowl and fork, six thin knitting needles or skewers, name labels and pencils, six short shoelaces.

What to do
Show the children what happens when you sandpaper the wooden block. (It makes sawdust.) Mix the mugs of sawdust and wallpaper paste and then add the water. Ask the children to help knead it into a workable dough, adding more water if necessary. Show them how to make beads (1.5cm diameter) by rolling the dough between the flattened palms of both hands. Push each 'bead' onto a named knitting needle and leave them to dry naturally (for three or four days). Thread the beads onto a shoelace and tie into bracelets.

Discussion
Hansel and Gretel's father made sawdust by the sawing action of cutting trees down.

What else can sawdust be used for? (Bedding for pet hamsters, or in making chipboard, for example.) In the past it was used to stop people slipping on floors (in a butcher's shop) and also for stuffing dolls. Some jewellery is worth a lot of money. What is jewellery made from? Perhaps it is made from gold or silver and contains precious stones.

For younger children
Give them a measured amount of dough to make each bead.

For older children
Help them to make very small beads, thread them onto very thin needles and secure with thread.

Follow-up activities
▲ Paint the beads and glaze them with PVA adhesive before threading.
▲ Add pieces of cut drinking straws and short pieces of macaroni to the sawdust beads. Arrange them into different patterns before threading to make a necklace.
▲ Flatten the sawdust dough and use pastry cutters to make different shapes. Push a hole through the shapes and when they are dry they can be threaded into pendants.
▲ Use sawdust dough to create a forest display (see 'In the forest', page 68).

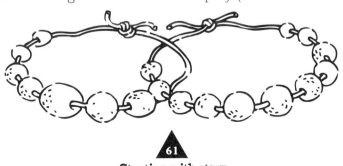

▲
61

Chocolate leaves

Objective
History – to find out when chocolate was discovered and to make chocolate leaves.

Group size
Four children.

What you need
Different sizes of evergreen leaves (for example, laurel, rhododendron, skimmia), bowl of soapy water, paper towels, 150g of cooking chocolate, palette knife, heat-resistant bowl, pan of water and source of heat.

Preparation
Collect the leaves, keeping the stalks as long as possible and wash them thoroughly in soapy water. Pat them dry on paper towels. Break up the chocolate into pieces and melt it in a bowl placed in a pan of water boiling on the stove (or for two minutes in a microwave oven). Be careful not to let the chocolate overheat and go lumpy. Work the melted chocolate into a smooth 'liquid' with a palette knife.

What to do
After the children have washed their hands, ask each child to select a leaf and then, holding it by the stalk, drag it slowly across the chocolate with the vein side down. Ensure the leaves are thickly coated underneath. It may be necessary to spread more chocolate using the palette knife. Try to avoid getting chocolate on the top side of the leaf, which makes peeling more difficult. When the chocolate has hardened (about 20 minutes), let the children peel the leaf away from it very carefully. Look at the imprint made in the chocolate leaf.

Discussion
What was the house in the forest that Hansel and Gretel found made of? (Sweets and chocolate.) A long time ago, in the sixteenth century, some explorers went to South America and discovered that the Aztec people made a drink from cocoa powder called 'chocolatl'. Cocoa powder comes from crushed cocoa beans which grow in pods on cacao trees. Chocolate gives you lots of energy but you have to be careful that the sugar in it doesn't spoil your teeth.

For younger children
Peel the leaves off for them to avoid the chocolate breaking.

For older children
Arrange the chocolate leaves on either side of a washed twig to look like a real tree branch.

Follow-up activities
▲ Make a collection of different kinds of wrappers from chocolate products.
▲ Try mixing cocoa powder with hot milk to make a drink. Is it easier to mix drinking chocolate?
▲ Find where South America is on a map of the world.

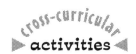

Way out

Objective
Geography – to move in the direction shown by arrows.

Group size
Whole group.

What you need
12 pieces of A4 cardboard, a thick black marker pen, eight chairs.

Preparation
Bend the pieces of card in half to make 'roof-top' signs and draw one large bold arrow on each card. Draw three arrows pointing north, three east, three west and three south.

What to do
Show the children the arrow cards and ensure they know what they are and that they show you which way to go. Let them have several practice turns in facing the direction that you show them on the arrows. The north arrow means go straight ahead. Ask them to help you dot the chairs around the room and place the prepared arrow cards on them so that they are pointing in different directions. The children can now take it in turns to walk round the room following the direction of the arrows.

Discussion
Where have the children seen arrows? (Car parks, hospitals, on road signs, for example.) If there had been arrows on the trees in the forest,

Hansel and Gretel would have been able to find their way home easily. Another way to tell the direction in which to go is by the position of the sun. Whereabouts in the sky is the sun at lunchtime each day? The midday sun shows you the way to the south – north is in the opposite direction. Where is the sun in the sky each morning when the children get up?

For younger children
Walk the 'chair route' with them to get them used to the idea of following the direction of arrows.

For older children
Keep changing the directions of the arrows on the 'chair route' to make it more challenging.

Follow-up activities
▲ Find the North and South Poles on a globe.

▲ Use the midday sun to decide which direction is south. Hold a magnetic compass in your hand and see how the needle always swings round to point in the direction of north whichever way you are facing. The other end of the needle always points south.

▲ On paper, draw arrows pointing north, south, east and west.

A pebble trail

Objective
Art – to practise using paint in small areas and to make a pebble trail.

Group size
Six children.

What you need
A bag full of small washed pebbles (bought from a garden centre or from a builder's merchant), a kitchen colander, a bowl of soapy water, paper towels, three containers of smooth white paint, a fine paintbrush for each child, plenty of newspaper, photocopiable page 94, coloured card.

Preparation
Wash the pebbles in soapy water, drain them through the colander and rinse them under running water. Leave them to dry thoroughly on the paper towels. Make six copies of photocopiable page 94 onto coloured card.

What to do
Lay newspaper over a table then ask the children to take a handful of pebbles each. Let them examine the pebbles before spreading them out on the newspaper in front of them. Ask them to paint as much of each pebble as they can without touching them with their fingers. They will have to leave the paint to dry before turning them all over and painting the other side. When the pebbles are completely dry, give each child a copy of photocopiable page 94 and see if they can lay a pebble trail to show Hansel and Gretel the way back home.

Discussion
Hansel and Gretel did not paint their pebbles so what made them show up in the dark? (The moonlight.) If you dig in the ground you will always find rocks and pebbles. They are important in a garden because they help soil drainage and are used as shelter for some creatures.

For younger children
Put the pebbles into a saucer of white paint and let the children stir them round with a fork to get them covered in white. Lift them out with the fork.

For older children
Stick the pebbles onto the photocopiable sheet with PVA adhesive to make a permanent trail.

Follow-up activities
▲ Estimate how many pebbles you would be able to carry in one of your pockets and then check to see if your guess was correct.
▲ Arrange the pebbles in groups, starting with one and adding one more each time – count them.
▲ Try 'writing' your initials using pebbles – how many do you need?

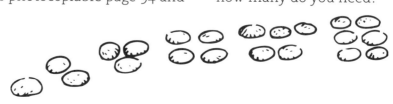

Sounds like a story

Objective
Music – to make percussion sounds to the story of Hansel and Gretel.

Group size
12 children.

What you need
A piece of sandpaper, a pair of shoes, a paper bag full of milk-bottle tops (pieces of foil), pebbles and a tea towel, a plastic bottle half full of pebbles, two telephone directories, a bunch of keys, a sheet of greaseproof paper and a piece of silver foil, an empty washing-up bottle, nailbrush and newspaper, a bag of small construction bricks.

What to do
Show the children the different sounds that can be made by using different objects (see below), then hand them out to them. While you read them the story of Hansel and Gretel suggest that they make sounds at particular moments in the story:

When the woodcutter is mentioned. (*Rub the sandpaper together in a sawing rhythm.*)
When the parents' plans are overheard. (*Make whispering noises.*)
When Hansel and Gretel creep out to collect pebbles. (*'Walk' the shoes very quietly on the floor.*)
When they walk through the forest. (*Shake the bottle-tops bag.*)
When Hansel secretly drops pebbles. (*Drop pebbles onto a tea towel.*)
When the parents leave Hansel and Gretel. (*Shake the bottle of pebbles for heavy feet crunching.*)
When the stepmother is furious. (*Bang your hands on the telephone directories.*)
When the bedroom door is locked and when Hansel is locked up. (*Jangle a bunch of keys.*)
When the father makes them a fire. (*Shake the greaseproof paper and the tin foil for crackling and burning sounds.*)
When the night sounds in the forest start. (*Hoot like an owl, squeeze the washing-up bottle for a mouse.*)
When the wind blows. (*Brush the newspaper.*)
When Hansel and Gretel grab the jewellery. (*Shake the bag of construction bricks.*)
When the oven door opens and slams. (*Open and close the door.*)
When Hansel and Gretel run back to their father. (*Beat hands on chest.*)

Discussion
If the children have ever been for a walk in the woods like Hansel and Gretel, what sounds did they hear? In bed at night, when most people are asleep, you can hear all sorts of sounds which you don't hear in the day – what are they? (Sounds made by central heating, the creaking of stairs, the hooting of owls, the noises of cats, for example.)

For younger children
Call them by name each time you want them to make 'their' sound.

For older children
Encourage them to make their sounds whenever they think it is appropriate in the story.

Follow-up activities
▲ Stand still, shut your eyes and listen to all the different sounds. Can you identify them?
▲ Blow recorders to see if you can make sounds like animals in the forest.

Hopping and skipping

Objective
PE – to move in ways which respond to mood and feeling.

Group size
Whole group.

What you need
The music of 'Skip to my Lou'. A piano or guitar (optional).

What to do
Ask the children to think about how they would have acted if they had been treated like Hansel and Gretel. What would they have done at the following moments in the story.

1 Their parents take them into the forest. (Dawdle and lag behind.)

2 They realise they have been left. (Try to find their way home by following the pebbles.)

3 They sit by the fire. (Huddle up together, warming themselves.)

4 They spy the house. (Skip.)

5 They realise it is made of sweets. (Help themselves.)

6 They slam the oven door on the wicked woman. (Run away quickly.)

7 They see all the woman's jewels. (Grab them to take home to their poor father.)

8 They find their father looking for them. (Jump for joy.)

Explain that you are going to sing some words and that they can move appropriately to the words of the song.

Sing the following verses, to the tune of 'Skip to my lou':

1 *Hansel and Gretel dragged their feet,*

Hansel and Gretel dragged their feet, Hansel and Gretel dragged their feet, when they were left in the forest.

2 *Hansel and Gretel tried to find home...*

3 *Hansel and Gretel warmed by the fire...*

4 *Hansel and Gretel skipped to the house...*

5 *Hansel and Gretel ate up the walls...*

6 *Hansel and Gretel grabbed all the jewels...*

7 *Hansel and Gretel ran away fast, Hansel and Gretel ran away fast,*
Hansel and Gretel ran away fast into the arms of their father.

Discussion
When you are in a strange place you can often feel frightened. Have the children ever been lost? When Hansel and Gretel ate parts of the candy house what should they have done first? (Asked permission.) Should they have taken the jewels?

For younger children
Show them the actions before each verse.

For older children
Sing the words while making the actions.

Follow-up activities
▲ Ask individual children to make one of the movements from the song. Can the others guess how they are feeling?

▲ Make facial expressions to show surprise, hunger, excitement, worry and happiness.

Skip to my lou!

Arranged by Peter Morrell

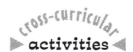
Toss the pancake

Objective
RE – to hear about the traditions of Lent, and to make a pancake.

Group size
Six children.

What you need
100g plain flour, 250ml milk, one egg, a pinch of salt, 50g butter, a mixing bowl and whisk, a frying pan and metal spatula, source of heat, sugar and a fresh lemon cut in half.

Preparation
Whisk all the ingredients (except the butter, sugar and lemon) in the bowl to make the pancake batter.

What to do
Tell the children that during the Christian festival of Lent some people eat only bread and drink water. This reminds them of what they've done wrong. On Shrove Tuesday, the day before Lent, people use up their eggs, flour and milk and make pancakes.

Show the children how to make pancakes. Heat a knob of butter in the frying pan so that all the surface is greased. Pour in enough batter to cover the base of the pan when it is tilted quickly. Loosen the pancake with the spatula and, holding the pan handle with both hands, flick the pan to toss the pancake onto its other side (ensure that the children are watching from a safe distance). When it's cooked, tip it onto a plate and the children can sprinkle it with sugar and

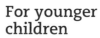

lemon juice. Fold it and let the children cut off pieces to eat. If you can manage to plop one pancake onto the floor, the children will never forget seeing pancakes made!

Discussion
The woman fed Hansel and Gretel with pancakes in her candy house. What other fillings could be put in a pancake? (Orange juice, jam, maple syrup, cheese.) Can the children name other foods which are made using milk, flour, eggs and butter? (Cakes, biscuits, puddings.) What food would they give up for Lent?

For younger children
Sprinkle the sugar for them to save gritty floors!

For older children
Let them weigh out and whisk the pancake batter.

Follow-up activities
▲ Say the rhyme 'Mix a pancake' in *This Little Puffin...* compiled by Elizabeth Matterson (Puffin).
▲ Paint a pancake onto a paper plate, cut it into pieces as if it had fallen on the floor. Then fit it together again.
▲ How many words can you think of to rhyme with Lent? (Bent, dent, gent, meant, scent, tent and so on.)

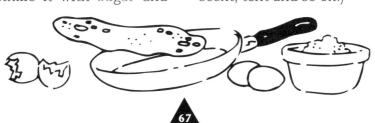

▲ **67**
Starting with story
Traditional story activities

In the forest

paper leaf matched to real leaf

sawdust-dough tree trunk

tree stump with sawdust scattered around

There is a [new] moon in the forest tonight

real leaf pinned to top of tree

finger-painted fire on paper

Group size
Six children at a time.

What you need
Dark-blue lining paper and a large piece of matching paper, green activity paper, corrugated and plain card, five pots of ready mixed paints: yellow, orange, red, brown, black, saucers for paint, circle template, silver paint, PVA adhesive and spreaders, Blu-Tack, marker pen, pencil, scissors, stapler. Fresh sawdust, wallpaper paste and water. Real leaves such as laurel, ivy, horse chestnut and lilac.

Preparation
Make sawdust dough (see 'Beads and bracelets', page 61) and shape long thin 'sausages', flatten them into tree-trunk shapes, leaving two of them short and stubby for stumps. Let the dough dry. Line the wall display area with dark-blue paper.

What to do
On the piece of blue paper, randomly fingerpaint the fire with different colours. Make leaf shapes on the green paper (see follow-up activities in 'Leafy clues', page 60) and cut them out. Draw shapes for a new moon, half moon and full moon on the card,

paint them silver and cut them out. Staple the fire to the middle of the display and arrange tree-trunks around it. Add some strips of corrugated card for branches and pin a real leaf to the top of each tree.

Ask the children to sort and match the paper leaves to each tree before sticking them onto the branches. Stick some fresh sawdust at the base of the tree stumps. Write a caption 'There is a____ moon in the forest tonight.' Write additional labels, 'new', 'half' and 'full'. Take one of the moon shapes to Blu-Tack into position and ask the children to choose the correct label for the caption.

Discussion
Although growing trees is very important, we sometimes need to cut them down to give other trees more room to grow or to provide wood to make things. How can you tell if a tree has been cut down recently? (The presence of sawdust.)

Follow-up activities
▲ Draw Hansel and Gretel, some woodland creatures and silver stars to add to the display.
▲ Collect some fallen leaves to add to the forest floor of the display.

The candy house

Group size
Six children.

What you need
A cardboard box (approximately 24cm x 24cm x 30cm), a piece of cardboard (50cm x 35cm), black paper, a craft knife (for adults), scissors, PVA adhesive and spreaders, a packet of paper hole reinforcements, split-pins, black envelope wrappers from wafer thin mint chocolates, a variety of other sweet and chocolate wrappers, a large cardboard sweet tube, labelling card and marker pen.

Preparation
Cut the top and bottom flaps off the box to leave only four walls. Cut out squares for windows and a door flap to open and shut. Score and bend the cardboard sheet in half for a roof and cut out a circle so that the cardboard tube will fit snugly.

What to do
Stick the chocolate envelopes onto the roof, overlapping them like tiles (cut more from black paper if necessary). Wedge the large sweet tube in the hole for a chimney. Stick paper hole reinforcements around the windows and doors to look like mints with holes. Cover the rest of the box with sweet wrappers using a chocolate bar cover for the door. Fix the cardboard roof to the box using split-pins and then label the box 'The candy house'.

Discussion
If the children were to stay in a candy house like Hansel and Gretel did, what sorts of problems might there be? If it was hot, the chocolate would melt. Perhaps the birds and animals would try to eat the house. Americans use the word 'candy' to mean sweets. Most sweets are made of sugar but in the past honey was used instead, and nuts and fruit were added.

Follow-up activities
▲ Put some doll's house furniture and play people inside the candy house and pretend that they are Hansel and Gretel.
▲ Count how many different types of sweet wrapper have been used in the display.
▲ Bake a sponge cake house and decorate it with chocolate-button roof tiles. Cover the walls with sugar-coated chocolate beans and jelly pastilles. Use liquorice type sweets for the door and chimney.
▲ Make some stuffed dates. Remove the stones and put marzipan in their place. Roll the dates in desiccated coconut.

The candy house

Bread and butter pudding

Group size
Six children.

What you need
Six medium slices of stale bread (200g), 60g butter, 100g dried apricots (or sultanas), 570ml milk, two eggs, 75g sugar, a 1-litre glass jug, handwhisk and spoon, spreading knife, chopping board and knife, large baking dish, piece of greaseproof paper.

Preparation
Buy the bread two or three days beforehand so that it will have had time to go stale. Grease the baking dish using a little of the butter and the greaseproof paper.

What to do
Show the children how to pull the crusts off the slices of bread and put them to one side. With the 'middles' of the slices ask them to make breadcrumbs by rubbing the bread between their fingers.

Cut the apricots into small pieces and add them to the crumbs. Break the eggs into the jug and whisk them with the sugar, gradually adding the milk. Pour this custard over the breadcrumbs in the baking dish, stir and leave to stand for half an hour while the breadcrumbs swell.

Tear the crusts into chunks, place them on top of the pudding and push them down gently. Dot the butter over the surface and bake in the oven at 180°C (350°F, Gas Mark 4) for about an hour, until the custard is set and the crusts have gone brown and crispy. Sit down and enjoy a portion of pudding each!

Discussion
Why couldn't Hansel and Gretel follow the trail of the breadcrumbs they had dropped? (The birds had eaten them.) What else do birds like to eat? (Worms, insects, seeds, nuts.) In winter, when the ground is frozen, it is important to feed the birds with tiny pieces of your own food, such as bacon rind and fat, or bits of cheese and apple.

Follow-up activities
▲ Place a bird-table near your window and put some wild bird seed on it. Draw the different kinds of birds that visit the table.
▲ Tie some string on a pine cone then dip it in some melted fat before rolling it in biscuit crumbs, peanuts, currants and breakfast cereals. Hang this bird cone outside and watch the birds peck at it.

The Emperor's New Clothes

The Emperor is too vain to admit that he cannot see his new clothes for fear of appearing stupid. Only a small boy is brave enough to speak up, revealing the true extent of the king's foolish pride as he parades naked through the streets to everyone's amusement. This humorous story shows that we should never be afraid to stand up for our principles.

Once upon a time there was an Emperor who spent all his time thinking about himself and his clothes. He had mirrors in every room to admire himself. Weavers and tailors grew rich selling him the latest fashions.

One day two rogues arrived and offered to make the Emperor an outfit with their magical cloth, which was invisible to anyone who was stupid. They measured him and showed him samples of stitching and fastenings. The Emperor gave them a workroom in the palace and some gold and silk thread.

After a few days, he visited the workroom, and the rogues said, 'Your majesty can see that your clothes are nearly ready.' The Emperor couldn't see anything, but because he didn't want to be thought stupid he agreed with them. He wanted to wear his new clothes for his birthday procession, so he sent his jester to see if they were ready. The jester didn't want to appear foolish either, and although he couldn't see the clothes he told the Emperor they would be ready soon.

On his birthday the Emperor went to the workroom. The rogues pretended to dress him with the new clothes, fastening the imaginary buttons and belt, but he could not see his new outfit. Of course, he didn't want to appear a fool, so he stood admiring himself in the mirror. All the courtiers told the Emperor how beautiful he looked – nobody wanted to appear a fool.

The Emperor mounted his horse and rode through the flag-lined streets with his soldiers marching alongside. Everyone had heard about the magical clothes and cheered and clapped – they didn't want to appear foolish. That is – everyone except one little boy, who had heard nothing. He asked his mother loudly, 'Why isn't the Emperor wearing any clothes?' The other children heard and asked their parents the same question. Soon everyone admitted that the Emperor was indeed naked and they laughed and laughed. Everyone made jokes about him at the street party which followed.

The Emperor realised how foolish he had been and that if the child had not been afraid to speak the truth he would have got colder and colder! He rushed back to his palace to get dressed and find the rogues. But they had already left, taking all the gold and silk thread with them.

Spots and stripes

Objective
English – to recognise and name different cloth patterns.

Group size
Six children.

What you need
Pieces of differently patterned fabric such as checks, stripes, spots, floral, starred, tartan, cord, silk, plain. A tray, two pieces of A4 card, scissors, PVA adhesive and spreaders.

Preparation
Cut small squares from the fabric (approximately 4cm) – at least six of each kind. Mix up all the pieces and put them on the tray. Cut the sheets of card into thirds lengthwise

then fold each strip in half and then into thirds. Open it out and fold it along the creases in concertina fashion to make a six-page zigzag book.

What to do
Hold up a piece of each patterned fabric and ask the children to describe it (not just by colour). Make sure that they know the words to describe it, for example 'checked' or 'striped'. Give them each a zigzag card strip and explain that they are going to make a pattern book. Ask them to find and take a floral piece of fabric from the tray and then to find a spotted piece, and so on until they each have all six pieces. Let them stick a piece of fabric onto each page of the zigzag book.

Discussion
Whenever the Emperor wanted new clothes he was shown a pattern book so that he could choose which kind of fabric he wanted them made from. Are the children allowed to choose their own clothes and are any of them made in fabrics similar to the ones in their pattern books? Which animals have stripes or spots? (Zebra, tiger, leopard, Dalmatian, thrush, for example.)

For younger children
Restrict the fabrics to four kinds and only make four folds on the card.

For older children
Ask them to fold their own zigzag book.

Follow-up activities
▲ Ask the children to find a particular fabric pattern and to fold their zigzag book in such a way that only that pattern page is showing.
▲ Use coloured crayons to copy the fabric patterns onto paper.
▲ Describe the clothes that your friend is wearing.
▲ Make a display with the patterns (see 'Fabrics and fasteners', page 85).

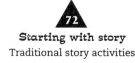

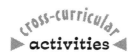

A stitch in time

Objective
English – to practise handwriting patterns.

Group size
Whole group for pattern practice then individual help for the worksheet.

What you need
A pair of denim jeans with heavy stitching on the back pocket, shoes or a handbag with top stitching, an article of clothing with decorative stitching. A marker pen and large sheet of paper, thick pencils and practice paper, photocopiable page 95 for each child, thick crayons.

What to do
Show the children the pattern of the pocket stitching on the jeans and point out the top stitching on the other articles. Explain that you want them to draw some stitches to make a pattern on the Emperor's cloak, but first they will need to practise.

Draw one of the cloak's patterns from photocopiable page 95 on a large sheet of paper and ask the children to copy the pattern with their finger in the air. Singing nursery rhymes at the same time will help to maintain their rhythm. Repeat this exercise with each of the writing patterns.

Let the children practise these stitching patterns on paper before using thick crayons to decorate the Emperor's cloak on the photocopiable sheet.

Discussion
The Emperor's clothes were made by sewing pieces of fabric together with stitches. Sometimes extra stitches are sewn, either to make the clothes stronger or to make them look more attractive. Why did the Emperor have extra stitching on his cloak? (To make it look very smart and important.) What other ways are there to decorate clothes? (Add beads and sequins and jewels, for example.)

For younger children
On the practice paper use a yellow highlighter pen to write out patterns for them to overwrite.

For older children
Let them make up their own patterns to go round the cloak edging and the crown on the photocopiable sheet.

Follow-up activities
▲ Stitch some patterns onto a piece of binca or open-weave J-cloth material.
▲ Make an outline of the Emperor's cloak on a piece of card. Punch holes in it and let the children sew in and out of the holes.
▲ Unpick the stitches of parts of a clean old shirt and show where the pieces had been stitched together.

Buttons and belts

Objective
Mathematics – to sort different types of fastenings into sets.

Group size
Six children.

What you need
A box of mixed buttons, large hooks and eyes, press-studs, zips, belts, pieces of Velcro, shoelaces, buckles, a shallow tray.

Preparation
Mix up all the different types of fastenings and put them in a tray.

What to do
Allow the children to handle and talk about the fastenings. Hold up one of each type and ask them to name it and tell you what it is used for. Encourage them to look at their own clothes to see if they have similar fastenings. Ask them to sort the fastenings from the tray into sets and then to name them, such as 'a set of hooks'. They may have sorted the buttons according to colour, size or the number of holes in them. This is fine as long as they can tell you the names of their set appropriately, such as 'a set of little buttons', 'a set of red buttons'.

Discussion
Do the children realise that all the items they have sorted are used for the same purpose of 'doing things up'? How would the Emperor's cloak have been fastened? (Invisible buttons or Velcro!) Sometimes zips catch, laces break or buttons come off clothes. When this happens what can be used for emergency fastenings? (Perhaps safety pins, string or elastic bands.) In the past, shoes were done up with buttons, and a special button hook was made to help fasten them.

For younger children
Limit the types of buttons to one colour, so that they can be sorted by size only.

For older children
Ask them to sort the buttons into subsets and tell you the name of the subset, giving as much detail as they can, such as 'a set of small, red buttons', 'a set of red buttons which have four holes'.

Follow-up activities
▲ Arrange the buttons in a repeating pattern and then thread them into a necklace.
▲ Say the nursery rhyme 'One two, buckle my shoe'.
▲ Practise tying shoelaces and fastening belts.

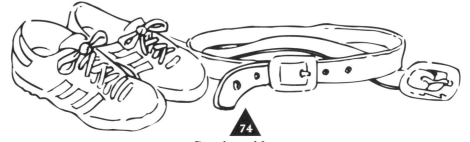

Made to measure

Objective
Mathematics – to measure height and discover how individual sizes vary.

Group size
The whole group then two children at a time for measuring.

What you need
Leftover rolls of wallpaper, scissors, pencils, a stapler.

Preparation
Remove any type of height measures from your room.

What to do
Explain to the children that you want to measure how tall they are and ask if they can think of a way of finding out. Proceed to put the children in pairs back to back, asking the others to say who is taller and who is shorter. Let them swap partners to compare themselves with other children and discover that they are taller than some and shorter than others.

Now two children at a time can make paper measurements. Roll the wallpaper out on the floor (plain side up) and ask one of the children to lie along the length of it with his head at the starting edge while the other child marks a pencil line on the paper where his feet reach. The measured child can then cut across the strip of paper and write his name along the top left edge of the plain side. When they (and you!) have cut out their own length, overlap the papers on the wall with the names showing and then staple them in position.

Discussion
Before the Emperor had his clothes made for him the tailors wanted to know his size. What parts of him would need to be measured? (His height, waist, length of arms and legs, neck and head.) Do the children know that you can tell the sizes of clothes by reading the label?

For younger children
If they can't write their name let them colour the corner of their paper for identification.

For older children
They can measure the length of their paper in centimetres and write this on the paper.

Follow-up activities
▲ How many measurement words can you think of? (Tall, long, high, short, wide...)
▲ Each child can draw round their foot onto paper and cut out the outline. Fix these paper feet 'walking' across the wall!
▲ Measure the room in footsteps. Do taller children take less steps than shorter ones?

Is that me?

Objective
Science – to look at and compare shiny surfaces and play a mime game.

Group size
Whole group.

What you need
A mirror on a stand, a hand mirror, several large spoons, a stainless steel teapot or dish, a biscuit-tin lid, some silver foil.

What to do
Ask each child to sit in front of the mirror in turn, put their hands on their head and tell the others what they can see. Explain that a mirror always reflects exactly what you do. Let the children look at themselves in all the different shiny surfaces, including the back and front of the spoons.

Put the children into pairs to play a mirror game. Name one of them to be the leader, the other to be the 'mirror' and ask them to kneel down facing each other. The leader makes an action and the 'mirror' has to copy the action exactly. For example, the leader positions her right hand and the 'mirror' has to position her left hand in the same way. When the leader has made several different movements it is time for the 'mirror' to have a turn at being the leader.

Discussion
The Emperor loved looking at the reflection of himself and had mirrors in every room in his palace. Were the children's reflections the same on all the shiny surfaces? In what other places can the children see reflections of themselves? (In puddles and ponds, car hub-caps, shop windows, pictures, in someone else's eyes, for example.)

For younger children
It will help younger children if you tell them the actions to make and if the directions are kept simple.

For older children
Suggest that they practise making different facial expressions to their 'mirror' – they can be as imaginative as they like!

Follow-up activities
▲ Shine a torch onto a hand mirror and then move the mirror just a little. See the torchlight bounce off the mirror onto another place. Pretend it is Tinkerbell the fairy moving round the room!

▲ Sit in front of a table mirror and hold the hand mirror behind your head. You will be able to see what the back of your hair looks like.

▲ Read the story of Snow White.

Crown the king

Objective
Design and Technology – to design a hat for a king.

Group size
Six children.

What you need
Coloured card (preferably gold or silver), pencils, scissors, PVA adhesive and spreaders, stapler, sticky tape, small buttons, sequins, silver foil, coloured Cellophane paper (sweet wrappers will do).

Preparation
Cut the card into strips measuring approximately 12cm wide and 65cm long. Cut small square and diamond shapes out of Cellophane paper.

What to do
Ask the children what sort of hat a king would wear and tell them you want them to design and make a suitable crown. First they will need to think about the edging. Should it be plain or wavy or spiked? Help them to draw their chosen pattern along the back edge of a card strip and ask them to cut it out.

Show them the other materials for them to choose 'jewels' to decorate their crown. The foil can be screwed up into silver balls. First they should arrange everything on the flat card before sticking it in place.

Finally, help them to staple the cardboard strip into a crown which will fit on their head. Cover the staples with a little sticky tape to prevent scratching.

Discussion
The Emperor wore a crown to show how important he was. Why do people wear hats? (For protection, for religious reasons, for decoration.) Some people wear helmets to protect themselves, such as soldiers, cyclists, police, miners, fire-fighters, builders and security guards. Sikhs wear turbans and Jewish men and boys wear yarmulkas. When it's hot we wear straw sun-hats and when it's cold we wear warm hats. Some girls and boys wear caps or straw boaters as part of their school uniform.

For younger children
Cut the card edge for them when they have decided on the pattern for their crown.

For older children
Let them cut their own shapes from the Cellophane paper.

Follow-up activities
▲ Design a tiara for a princess to wear.
▲ Play a game of musical hats. Whenever the hat is put on your head, move it quickly on to someone else's. Whoever is wearing the hat when the music stops is out!

▲ **77**
Starting with story
Traditional story activities

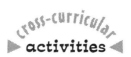

Court jester

Objective
History – to find out about court jesters and make a harlequin pattern.

Group size
Six children.

What you need
Different-coloured gummed paper sheets, scissors, pencil and ruler, a piece of card for a template, a sheet of white A4 paper for each child, three pieces of wetted sponge on saucers.

Preparation
Draw a rectangle 7cm x 5cm on the card and rule a diamond shape inside it. Cut out the shape and use this as a template to make the diamond shapes from the coloured gummed paper. You will need about 15 diamonds for each child – several can be cut together.

What to do
Show the children the cardboard template and ask them if they know what shape it is. Invite them to count how many sides the diamond has. Does it remind them of any other shapes – two triangles stuck together or a slanting square?

Give them a sheet of paper each and let them pick out some gummed diamond shapes. Show them how to arrange the shapes so that they will fit together and then let them arrange their own on the paper to make a harlequin pattern. The diamonds can be stuck in place by wetting the gummed surface on the sponges.

Discussion
The Emperor lived in a palace with his courtiers (helpers). One of them was the court jester or fool, whose job it was to make the Emperor laugh by telling him jokes and fooling around. A court jester was dressed in harlequin (multicoloured diamond-patterned) tights, wore a three-cornered hat with bells on each point and carried a special stick called a bauble. Who else makes people laugh? (A clown, a comedian or an actor in a pantomime.)

For younger children
Give them half a sheet of paper so that they will only need to arrange and stick seven diamond shapes.

For older children
Make several cardboard templates for them to draw and cut out their own diamond shapes.

Follow-up activities
▲ Sing the nursery rhyme 'Twinkle twinkle little star'.
▲ Make each other laugh by telling jokes or 'clowning around'.
▲ Take the joker from a pack of playing cards, hide it somewhere in your room and play 'Hunt the jester'.
▲ Make a jester's bauble out of card and attach it to a plant cane.

Flying the flag

Objective
Geography – to look at different flags and make them into bunting.

Group size
Whole group.

What you need
Pictures of world flags, a hand-held Union Jack (from a toy shop or stationers), sheets of white A4 paper, pencils, scissors, thick and thin crayons, ruler, sticky tape, string.

Preparation
Fold a piece of A4 paper into four and copy different flag markings into each rectangle. Photocopy several sheets and then cut out the flags. Cut the string into 1-metre lengths.

What to do
Show the children the Union Jack flag and explain that it is displayed and waved whenever there is a celebration such as the Queen's birthday. Hold up the pictures of world flags and point out how each country uses different colours and that some have different stripes – vertical, horizontal and diagonal. See if they can recognise and name the shapes of stars, crescents, circles and triangles.

Hand out the photocopied flag pictures and ask the children to colour at least one flag each. Help them to make a narrow fold on the shortest side, slip the string inside and tape the fold over the string. Do this with each of the flags so that they all hang on the string to form a length of bunting. Hang it up in your room.

Discussion
On the day of the Emperor's birthday procession the buildings and streets were decorated with strings of flags called bunting. A flag is used as the symbol for a country, and each country has a different arrangement of colours on its flag. Can the children think of other examples where colours are used to represent different things? (Football strips, the colour-coding of books in a children's library.) Why is a red flag sometimes displayed on a beach? (To warn of danger.)

For younger children
Colour in small sections on the flag for them to copy the colours.

For older children
Let them mark out and colour a flag of their own choice.

Follow-up activities
▲ Use the bunting in a display (see 'The big procession', page 84).
▲ Stick coloured tissue-paper strips to a wooden spoon and use it as a paper waver.
▲ Mark out your own personal flag, colour it and fix it to a plant cane.

On parade

Objective
Art – to look at the colours of soldiers' uniforms and to paint a peg soldier.

Group size
Four children.

What you need
Pictures or toy models of soldiers in ceremonial uniforms and in khaki. Red, blue, orange, yellow and brown paint in pots with fine brushes, an unsprung wooden clothes peg (from hardware shops) and a pipe-cleaner for each child, a fine black felt-tipped pen, some Plasticine.

Preparation
Mix yellow and brown paint until it resembles the dull yellowish-brown colour of khaki.

What to do
Show the children the two soldiers, in different dress from each other, and discuss the different tasks they carry out (see Discussion). Give each child a blob of Plasticine for them to make into a squashed ball. This is to be the stand for their soldier.

Ask the children to choose which type of soldier they would like to paint and give them one of the wooden pegs. The ceremonial soldier can have blue legs, a red jacket and hat and orange buttons. The foot soldier should be khaki all over.
When the paint is dry, pen in the face features and wrap the pipe-cleaner around the

peg for arms. Stand the soldiers in the Plasticine.

Discussion
At his birthday procession the Emperor was surrounded by all his soldiers marching along. What jobs do soldiers do? (They provide defence for a country.) Soldiers who have to be ready for attack wear khaki-coloured uniform, so that they are camouflaged and can't be seen. Soldiers who guard the Queen at Buckingham Palace wear tall fur hats called busbies.

For younger children
Hold the peg for them while they paint the soldier's uniform.

For older children
Let them mix the khaki paint themselves.

Follow-up activities
▲ Read the poems 'At Home' and 'Buckingham Palace' by AA Milne in *When We Were Very Young* (Mammoth).
▲ Make different creatures using wooden spring pegs. Draw features on the face and add fabric and paper scraps.
▲ Slot the peg soldiers onto the edge of a tin and use them for adding and take-away practice.
▲ Sing 'The Guard Song' from *Appuskidu* (A & C Black).

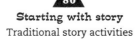

Left, right, left, right

Objective
Music – to play a marching game to the rhythm of a drum.

Group size
Whole group.

What you need
A drum and beaters or tambourine. If neither are available, use an upturned biscuit tin with your hand or a wooden spoon beater.

What to do
Beat the drum and ask the children to take steps in time to the beats. Let them practise listening and responding to the rhythm of the drumbeat by marching and swinging their arms.

Now show them which is their left foot and ask them to start marching with that foot each time they hear the drum. Explain that you are going to play a marching game which depends on them listening carefully to the drumbeat and keeping in step with the leader.

Choose two children to follow you as you beat the drum and march round the room. Each time you have been round the room, pick two more children to join in marching behind you until eventually the whole group is included.

As each child joins the march they should adjust their steps to be in time with the others. You can move all over the room in an 's' or zigzag pattern. Make sure the children have straight backs, heads held high and arms swinging as they march like soldiers.

Discussion
At the Emperor's birthday procession the soldiers marched as they guarded him. The beat of the drum helped them all to keep in step. Why is it important for soldiers to march in step and move at the same speed? (So that they don't fall over each other.)

For younger children
Let them join in the march starting with either foot.

For older children
Let them take turns in beating the drum and being the leader.

Follow-up activities
▲ Sing and march to 'The Grand Old Duke of York' from *Oranges and Lemons* compiled by Karen King (Oxford University Press).
▲ Practise which is left and right by playing a game of 'Hokey Cokey'.
▲ March to other percussion instruments.

Try it on

Objective
PE – to develop physical skills through mime and role-play.

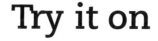

Group size
Five children.

What you need
The dressing-up clothes hanging on coat hangers on a rack, a tape-measure, long mirror, 12 chairs, two tables, three pieces of A4 card, scissors, marker pen.

Preparation
Cut each sheet of card into quarters and write a large number 1, 2, 3 or 4 on each, so that you have three of each number. If you don't have a rack for the dressing-up clothes, you could use a low cupboard and hang the clothes on the doors.

What to do
Tell the children that you are going to make some shop changing rooms and let them help to arrange the chairs to make three little cubicles. Place the mirror outside the 'changing rooms' and put the number cards on a table next to the mirror. Position the clothes rack by the table.

To begin with explain to the children that you are going to pretend that you are putting on some different types of clothes. Just like the Emperor, the children won't be able to see their clothes!

Ask the children to copy you as you mime stretching and bending, pulling and squeezing to put on your new clothes. When the children have put on their 'clothes' they should twirl and parade like the Emperor did. Encourage them to explore different 'dressing-up' movements.

Now let the children use the shop environment for role-playing. One child can be the shop assistant who should give the customers the relevant numbered card to match the number of items they want to try. This assistant can also help measure any customers who don't know what size they are! Another child can put the clothes back on the rack afterwards. The other three children can be the customers who pick the clothes off the rack for trying on.

Discussion
Before you buy new clothes you need to know that they are going to fit you, and this is why you need to try them on. If you are having clothes made for you like the Emperor, you need your measurements taken first. The assistant in the shop gives you a number card to make sure that all the clothes are returned.

For younger children
Help them to dress and undress.

For older children
Let them make the number cards.

Follow-up activities
▲ Make a chart showing which children are able to perform dressing tasks such as buttoning coats, zipping jackets, tying shoelaces and turning clothes back from inside out.
▲ Dress the dolls in clothes which would be suitable for the Emperor's procession.

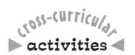

Joseph's coat

Objective
RE – to listen to a story about Joseph and to colour his coat by numbers.

Group size
Eight children.

What you need
Photocopiable page 96 for each child, a variety of felt-tipped pens and crayons to include the following colours: pink, blue, green, yellow, red, orange, purple and brown. A picture bible story book such as *The Children's Illustrated Bible*, retold by Selina Hastings (Dorling Kindersley). A piece of card (50cm x 20cm) and thick marker pen.

Preparation
Write the numbers 1 to 8 spaced out on the card and colour a patch underneath each number according to the following key: 1 – pink, 2 – blue, 3 – green, 4 – yellow, 5 – red, 6 – orange, 7 – purple, 8 – brown.

What to do
Tell the children the story of Joseph, who was his father Jacob's eleventh son. Because he was the favourite his brothers were very jealous of him, and when Jacob gave him a coat of many colours they hated him even more. Tell the children more about Joseph and his brothers from a bible story book.

Ensure that the children can recognise the numbers 1 to 8 and know the names of the colours on the key. Give them each a copy of photocopiable page 96 and ask them to colour the sections that are numbered 1 in pink. They should then find the sections numbered 2 and colour them in blue. Go through all the colours and ask the children to complete the sheet.

Discussion
Joseph's coat was very precious to him, and the Emperor thought that his new cloak made by the rogues would be just as special. Why was he disappointed? When clothes are made of pieces of coloured material sewn together it is called patchwork.

For younger children
Colour a little corner of each section on the coat for them to copy.

For older children
Ask them to make their own key card for their photocopiable sheet.

Follow-up activities
▲ Experiment by mixing paint colours together – red and yellow makes orange, black and white makes grey, yellow and blue makes green, red and blue makes purple.
▲ Draw eight curved lines in a rainbow arch and colour the bands red, orange, yellow, green, blue, indigo and violet.
▲ Find out which colour is the most popular among the children.

The big procession

Group size
Four children at a time.

What you need
Blue frieze paper, gold card, coloured and white activity paper, thin pink and white card, corrugated card, thick string, peg soldiers (see 'On Parade', page 80), bunting (see 'Flying the flag', page 79), scissors, pencils, felt-tipped pens, stapler, labelling pen.

Preparation
Line the display area with the frieze paper. Make some thought bubbles out of white card.

What to do
Cut spikes, rectangles and dome shapes out of gold card and staple them to the top of the display to look like a palace in the background. Try stuffing paper behind them so that they look three-dimensional. Fix the string across the display area and peg the soldiers onto it.

Let the children share the following tasks: draw some people, colour them and cut them out; cut the Emperor out of pink card; make a paper jester and colour his tights in a harlequin pattern; draw and cut out a drummer boy and a horse; make a tree from corrugated card and place the boy who was 'brave enough to speak out' on one of the branches.

Ask the children what the people would be thinking when they saw the naked Emperor ride by on his horse, then help them to write the people's thoughts into the bubbles made from white card. Staple the people and their thought bubbles onto the display. Fix some bunting round then label it 'The Emperor's birthday procession'.

Discussion
Everybody at the procession knew that the Emperor wasn't wearing any clothes but if they had said anything they would have appeared foolish, so they kept their thoughts to themselves. Why did the little boy dare to say out loud what he could see?

Follow-up activities
▲ Group the soldiers into pairs and practise the beginning of the two-times table. Say and show that 1 x 2 makes 2, 2 x 2 makes 4, and 3 x 2 makes 6.
▲ Make some party foods and have a pretend street party.

Fabrics and fasteners

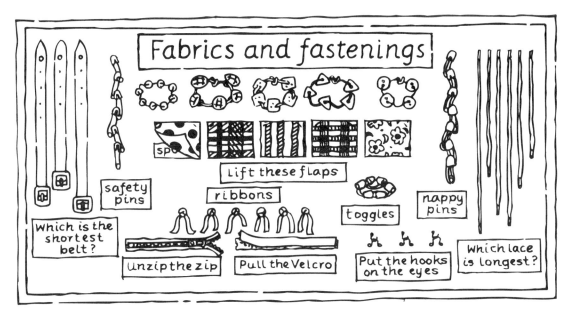

Fabrics and fastenings

Which is the shortest belt?

safety pins

Lift these flaps

ribbons

Unzip the zip

Pull the Velcro

toggles

Put the hooks on the eyes

nappy pins

Which lace is longest?

Group size
Six children.

What you need
A display board covered in neutral, textured material, a box of mixed buttons, 6cm x 20cm lengths of coloured ribbons, six tapestry needles and wool, rectangular pieces of spotted, striped, checked, floral, and tartan fabric, shoelaces, belts, a 30cm zip, hooks and eyes, a 10cm piece of Velcro, nappy and safety pins, hook pins or drawing pins, stapler, labelling card and marker pen.

Preparation
Thread six needles with wool and make a large knot at the end. Attach the nappy pins to each other and do the same with the safety pins.

What to do
Ask the children to sort the buttons into types, for example large, small, shiny, blue, red, bobble. Ask them to thread a few of their buttons onto the wool and then help them to tie them into a loose bracelet and hook them across the top of the display.

Hang the shoelaces down one side of the display board and the belts down the other side. Staple the zip, the back piece of Velcro and the hooks (from the hooks and eyes) across the bottom where the children can reach them. They can then unzip the zip, add the top piece of Velcro and hang the 'eyes' on the hooks.

Fix the rectangles of fabric across the middle of the board so that they can be lifted to show their label underneath. Help the children to make double knots in the ribbons and add these 'bows' to the display. Hang up the 'strings' of pins and label everything in the display.

Discussion
Most clothes have some type of fastener. Some shorts, pants and skirts are held up using elastic in the waistband, instead of a belt. Do the children have any fasteners on their clothes? Which are the easiest to use? Are they wearing fabrics which match the display?

Follow-up activities
▲ Use the display to count buttons, learn the names of fabrics, operate some of the fastenings and to assess shortest and longest.
▲ Cut up small pieces of fabric and push them with a pencil into a polystyrene lid to make a multicoloured collage.

Puffy wuffy pudding

Group size
Six children.

What you need
A tin of evaporated milk (170g), one packet of strawberry jelly (135g), a kettle of water, hand-held electric or rotary whisk, a large mixing bowl, a 1-litre glass measuring jug, tin opener, fork, plastic bowl, spatula, six clean empty yogurt pots, coloured sugar strands ('Hundreds and thousands').

What to do
Ask the children to wash their hands, separate the jelly into cubes and put the pieces into the glass jug. Pour 300ml of boiling water onto the jelly pieces which the children can then stir (under careful supervision) with the fork until the jelly has dissolved.

Put the jelly into the fridge to cool and leave it until it is just setting, which takes about three-quarters of an hour (time it carefully). You can tell it is ready when it coats the side of the jug when tipped. (If the jelly sets before you 'catch' it, place the jug into a bowl of hot water to melt it slightly again.) Meanwhile let the children take it in turns to whisk the evaporated milk until it is thick and bulky and then whisk in the setting jelly. Spoon the puffy wuffy pudding into the yogurt cartons, decorate it with the sugar strands and enjoy eating it!

Discussion
After the Emperor's birthday procession all his subjects had a huge street party. They brought chairs and tables onto the street and all sat down together to eat party food. The children loved the puffy wuffy pudding the best! What else do people eat at parties? What kind of games do the children play at their birthday parties?

Follow-up activities
▲ Weigh the milk, jelly and water before you begin and compare this to the weight of the finished dessert.

▲ The jelly disappeared in the water; see what happens when sugar or salt is stirred into water. Try this same experiment with hot water – does it make any difference?

▲ Soak some marrowfat peas in water overnight. Where does the water go?

▲ **86**
Starting with story
Traditional story activities

'T' for turnip

▲ Write in the beginning letter.

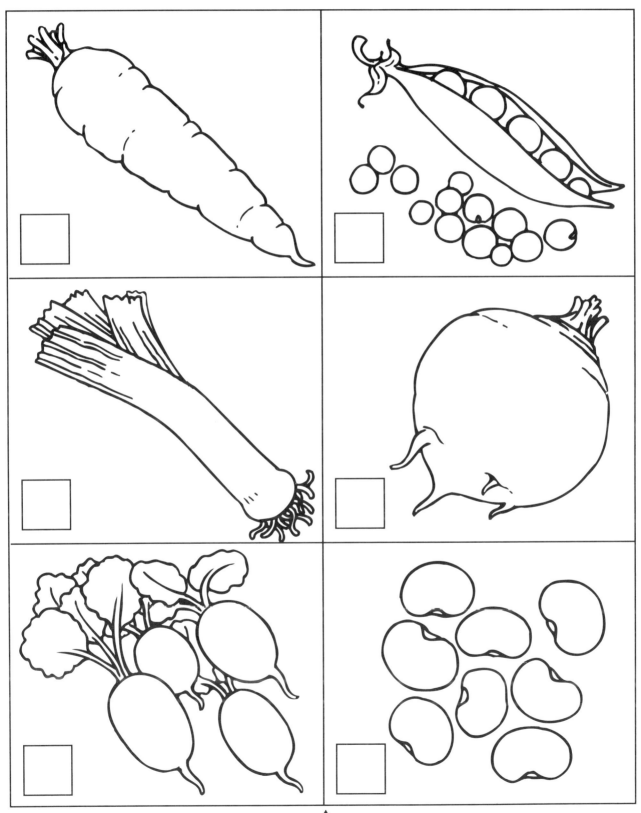

Which order?

Listen to this!

▲ Colour the characters and write their names.

Starting with story
Traditional story activities

Foxy

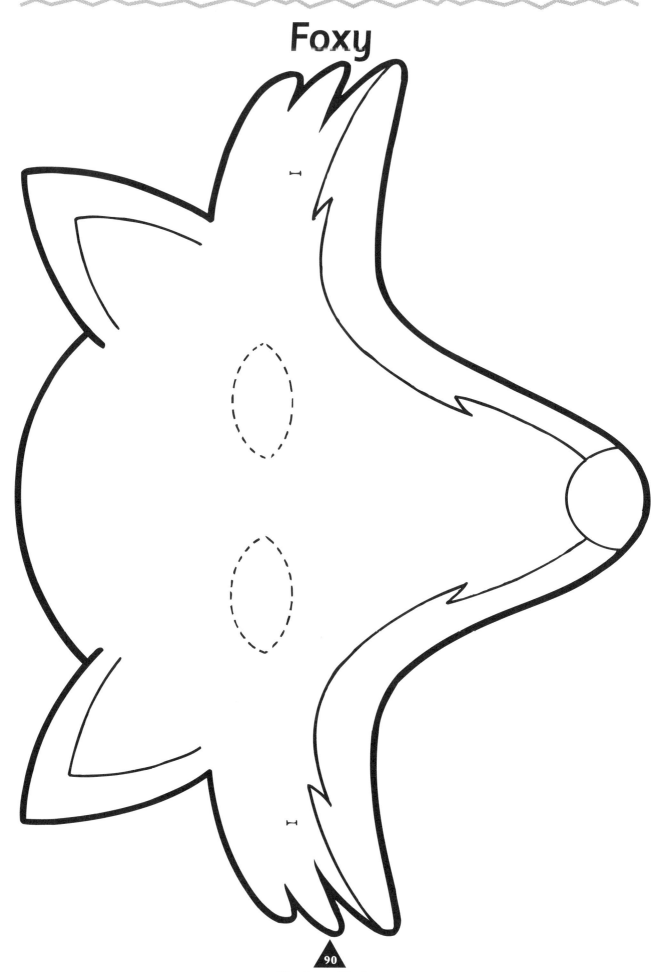

Starting with story
Traditional story activities

Plaits and rope-ladders

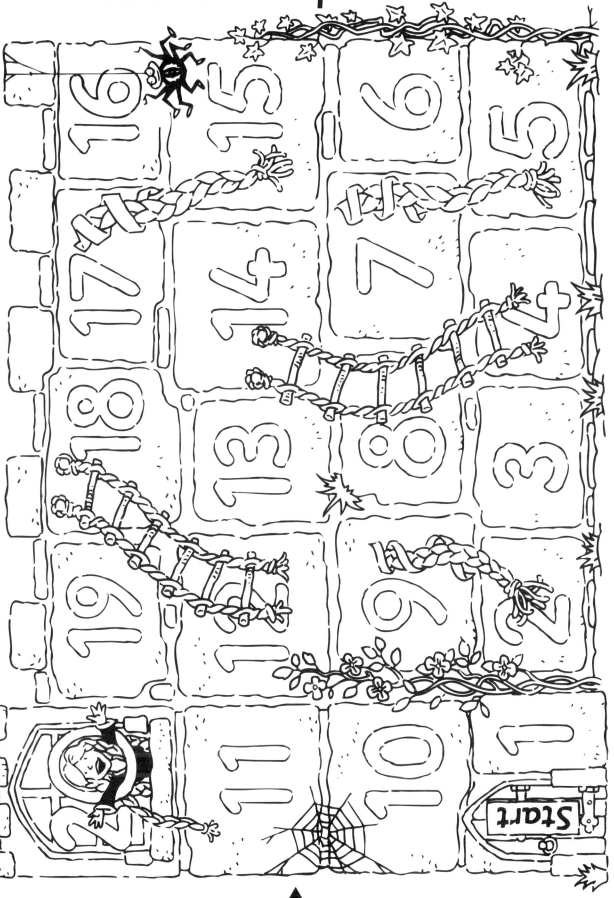

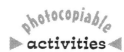

A dotty alphabet

▲ A dotty alphabet – push a pencil point through the dots.

A   B   C   D   E   F   G

H   I   J   K   L   M   N

O   P   Q   R   S   T   U

V   W   X   Y   Z

Leafy clues

▲ Draw a circle around the odd one out and finish
the picture.

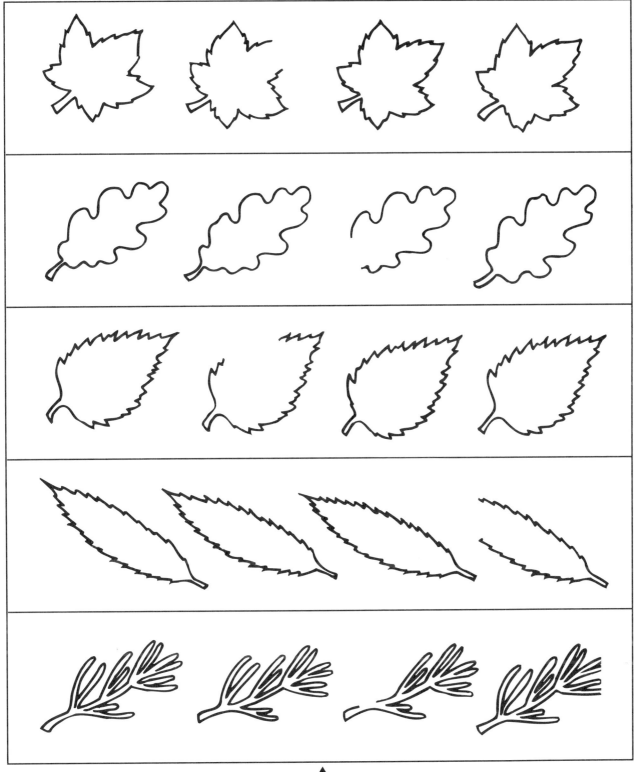

A pebble trail

▲ Place your pebbles to make a trail back home.

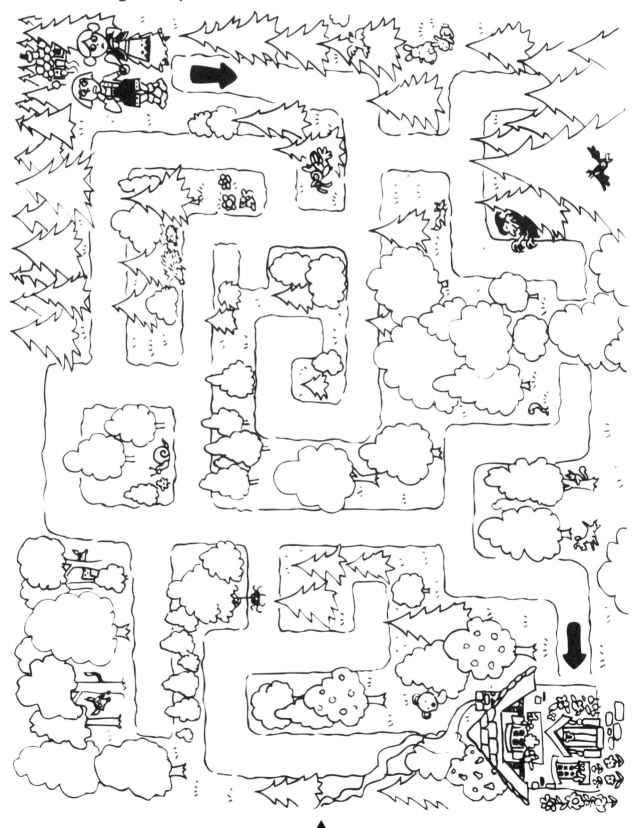

A stitch in time

▲ Draw the patterns on the Emperor's cloak.

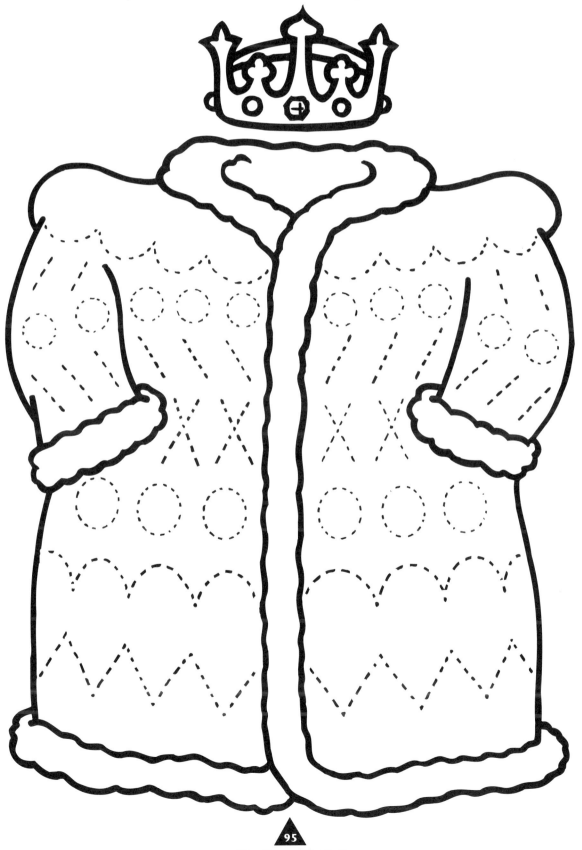

Joseph's coat

▲ Use the colour key numbers to complete Joseph's coat.

Key
1 pink
2 blue
3 green
4 yellow
5 red
6 orange
7 purple
8 brown